Reflections on Mind and the Image of Reality

Reflections on Mind and the Image of Reality

Jason Brown

RESOURCE *Publications* · Eugene, Oregon

REFLECTIONS ON MIND AND THE IMAGE OF REALITY

Copyright © 2017 Jason Brown. All rights reserved. Except for brief quotations in critical publications or reviews, no part of this book may be reproduced in any manner without prior written permission from the publisher. Write: Permissions, Wipf and Stock Publishers, 199 W. 8th Ave., Suite 3, Eugene, OR 97401.

Resource Publications
An Imprint of Wipf and Stock Publishers
199 W. 8th Ave., Suite 3
Eugene, OR 97401

www.wipfandstock.com

PAPERBACK ISBN: 978-1-5326-1690-7
HARDCOVER ISBN: 978-1-4982-4093-2
EBOOK ISBN: 978-1-4982-4092-5

Manufactured in the U.S.A. MAY 23, 2017

To my children and for the world I hope they will inherit

"I yearn towards some philosophic song

Of Truth that cherishes our daily life."

WORDSWORTH, PRELUDE 230-1

Contents

Preface | xi

PART I: The Rational Animal | 1

    The Study of the Mind | 3

    Reflexivity | 6

    Subject, Self, Object | 10

    Concepts and Categories | 14

    Change, Replication and Process | 18

    Between Moments | 23

    Experience | 26

    Meaning in Life | 32

    Thought and Memory | 36

    The Simple and the Complex | 41

    Depth | 43

    Absence | 47

    Variables | 49

    Repression and Denial | 52

    All the World's a Stage | 56

Contents

PART II: The Emotional Animal | 61

    Otherness | 63

    On Love | 69

    Compassion | 74

    Will | 76

    Drive | 78

    Feeling and Emotion | 80

    Wish and Desire | 83

    Asceticism | 90

    Hedonism | 94

    Narcissism | 98

    Illusion and Conviction | 101

    God | 106

    Spirit | 109

    Mysticism | 111

    Atheism | 113

    Optimism | 116

PART III: The Political Animal | 121

    Conflict | 123

    Adaptation | 126

    Freedom | 128

    Value | 134

    Adapting to Society | 137

    Globalization and Cultural Identity | 140

    Wholeness and Alienation | 145

Contents

The Call of the Wild | 150

Politics | 154

Justice and the Law | 158

Duty | 162

Lying | 165

Character and Personality | 169

Reflection and Expectation | 172

PART IV: The Imaginative Animal | 177

Writing | 179

Cultural Mythology | 183

Art and Philosophy | 187

Creativity | 190

Truth and Objectivity | 194

Reason | 196

Education | 198

My Library | 203

Phrenology | 206

PART V: Concluding thoughts | 209

Concentration and Meditation | 211

On Falling Asleep | 213

The Examined Life | 217

Psychoanalysis and the Family | 220

Endowment | 224

Looking Back and Regret | 226

Aging and Death | 230

Preface

There is nothing stable in the world; uproar's your only music
JOHN KEATS ("TO GEORGE AND THOMAS KEATS, JANUARY 13, 1818")

This collection of brief essays and still briefer commentaries is a personal reflection on some topics that have been thematic in the development of my theoretical work. These essays are not meant to extend the theory into yet-uncharted territory, but rather to draw out some of its implications for clinical neuroscience, philosophy of mind and everyday life. The point of view guiding these reflections can be found in prior works, but the discerning reader will not fail to see a departure from current models of mind and brain based on circuit board diagrams, modular and computational theories that conflict with a processual account in which the mind/brain is more like a living organism. This perspective, which is often at odds with common sense and folk psychology, has particular relevance to our concepts of the self, the inner life, subjective time, adaptive process and the world represented in perception[1].

The work also takes up, sympathetically, the concept that our strongest beliefs are illusory: the self, free will, the object world, indeed, all conscious experience. In that mind is an outcome of brain activity, with all experience—internal and external—occurring as mental phenomena, it is inarguable that, aided by sensation, the brain creates a changing picture of

---

1. For a better understanding of the theory behind these essays, the reader is referred to a recent book for discussion and references: *Microgenetic Theory and Process Thought*, Imprint Academic, Exeter 2015

Preface

the world, along with inner states and a feeling of realness in relation to mental content. Dreams, thoughts, feelings, images, memories, seem more or less real though images are less real than objects, decisions less real than acts, except for those who live resolutely in a world of ideas.

I would also take this opportunity to express my good fortune over the years for the friendships and conversations with David Bradford, John Cobb, Marcel Kinsbourne, Maria Pachalska, Karl Pribram, Michael Trupp, Don Tucker and Michel Weber, as well as many others, for the fellowships and grants from NIH, the Foundation's Fund, a Humboldt stipendium and other sources to study in various laboratories, and my gratitude to those mentors and colleagues with whom I have worked, especially Norman Geschwind in Boston, Henri Hecaen in Paris, Anton Leischner in Bonn, A. R. Luria in Moscow and George Miller in New York. Though now largely forgotten, they were, in the day, right or wrong, whether in agreement or contention, the best in their fields. There is also a particular debt to process thinkers and idealist philosophers of the recent past, in whose work the theory found a philosophic home, especially Bergson, James, Bradley, Whitehead, Sprigge, and certain of the German Romantics, though the theory matured largely in the context of work on clinical phenomena.

Jason Brown
New York
www.drjbrown.org

PART I

The Rational Animal

How can we reconcile a world in flux with a self that is relatively constant?

The Study of the Mind

To know yourself is risky. The unconscious is a sleeping dog that bites.

CAN WE SAY THAT within the brain a world of appearance governs the whole of our lives? The distinction of real and phenomenal for an individual perspective is a distinction of a physical brain and a phenomenal world. This enables the organism, with the aid of sensibility, to navigate a surround of other entities, organisms and physical brains; a world that can be apprehended by visual or auditory perception; tactile and olfactory modalities; each of which—conscious or not—mirrors a reality that approximates some or many features of real entities. It is an act of faith or a core belief that the world we perceive is physically real or aligned with the image it portrays. The simplest proof of this is the motor and perceptual lag in consciousness by which we know that the appearance of the world is off-line with mind-independent events.

We imagine a real world beyond our own, but the image that exists in the mind is not a screen to what is physically real. The organism that adapts to a physical world becomes ingredient in that world, part of the Umwelt that will influence the evolutionary path of other organisms. Primitive mind orients the organism in a daily struggle to live. Advanced mind evolves as the Umwelt becomes an expanded functional space, with novel dangers and opportunities. Organism and mentality are part of this space and a surrogate of the absence which they now occupy.

Consider this analogy. We blow up a child's balloon to a certain shape. Is the shape of the balloon the container or is it the air inside, or the "empty" space it replaces or the configuration in the brain it arouses? Or again, we reach into the world as a hand is inserted into a glove. The fit is perfect though hand and glove are different kinds of things. We see the

Reflections on Mind and the Image of Reality

gloved hand, but we feel the actual hand. We accept a hand, gloved or not, as a mental image, and suppose real flesh and blood within the image to which it corresponds. The hand shapes the glove; the glove constrains and configures the hand. Is this a useful metaphor for mind and brain, or sensibility and appearance? Is the world like an extended skin that surrounds a physical organ? The brain is derived from ectoderm, like the skin. Cortex and skin are multi-layered, with bottom-up development; the skin sheds the outer dead layer; the brain sheds objects that become independent.

Think of the hand as a brain, and the glove as a perceptual model. My image of a scene overlaps that of my neighbor because the scene is in my head, not out there. Similarly, we can ask: is the physical world that which is represented by the brain, or is it more like a 3-D film with nothing behind it? To what does the imaginary world correspond? We move about in this world as if in a dream, a world elaborated by the brain which—as in the relation of hand to glove—points outward to a physical world and inward to the physical hand/brain. The flesh and blood of the hand, the cells and connectivity of the brain: that is where the real correlate of the image is to be found.

We understand that every object has many modes of existence. A chair is a perceptual object that "stands for" a physical entity. The chair is independent of the different perspectives by which it is perceived. It is a member of a category of functionally and spatially related objects as well as a pattern of brain activity. Finally, it exists as the constituent molecules that compose it. The dilemma is that the perceptual model or appearance of the chair so dominates our beliefs so that what we see seems to be what there is. The most parsimonious way to think about an object is to note that what we see is obviously wrong. The problem, which arises with consciousness, has the corollary that my existence is predicated on the consciousness that I exist. This does not mean there is no existence as a sleeping or comatose entity, but that the I, or consciousness, is part of my existence. If to exist means to be conscious of existing, and if the brain cannot be said to be conscious, my existence as a physical entity, if not a conscious one, requires consciousness.

In human mind, adaptation goes beyond the reconciliation of appearance and the physical world. The mind apprehends and acts. The self adapts to changing conditions. This is a higher form of adaptation in which an illusory self adapts to an illusory world apart from brain correlates and without a necessary correspondence to immediate events in the world. The illusion of self and appearance arises in brain, but the world has a double aspect. To say, the self does not exist is plausible; to say the world does not exist seems absurd. This is because we believe there is a correspondence of (the illusion of) the self to some pattern of brain activity, while objects appear independent of mind and brain.

∽

The I is the agent, the me is the object. The me is wider, more persistent (recurrent) than the I, which is its momentary specification.

When we say, I hurt (amuse, upset etc.) myself, the me is an object of actions of the I.

The conscious self can undergo rapid change, angry one moment, placid the next, while change in the me is glacial.

A momentary self, the I, passes to another I, but the me recurs with minor change.

The me doesn't initiate, it receives. The active and passive exemplars of the self correspond to agency and character.

The me is the object of self-perception; the I is the self that perceives. The conscious self presumes to know the unconscious self, which is not so much observed as extracted from the sum of its beliefs and acts.

Could the unconscious self be an artifact of its categorical nature embracing, as potential, all possible implementations in a momentary I?

The momentary self, the I, is conscious because it specifies the category of the me, which is the sum of all specifications.

In Moscow they said, talk theory for 5 hours; in Boston, 15 minutes for data. Eventually, the conclusion was in the title of the paper, the rest being superfluous.

If you say red and I say blue, there is nothing to debate. If you say a strong red and I say a weak one, the fight is on. The category is critical.

Reflexivity

Without illusion, reality could not be inferred.
Without reality, life would be a perpetual dream.

THE SELF IS CONSCIOUS of objects and inner states but to what extent is consciousness of self possible? If not, what does it mean to say the self is conscious of something if there is no consciousness of self? Things that appear real are images, and a feeling of realness can be more vivid in a hallucination or in a dream. In dream, we may ask, is this real, but this is rare in wakefulness. And so, most expressions of thought are not just artifacts of language but often self-referential problems inherent in the nature of mind. There is a reflexive quality in such problems as self and non-self, illusion and reality, subjective and objective.

Consider that mind is elaborated by brain but the brain and its activity are inferred from an image in the mind. We live in the present but the present is a step behind the real. Our response to events begins before we are conscious of them. Remembrance is a present experience with a feeling of pastness, yet the present, though not felt as past, is already a memory. If the duration of the present is illusory, how can it be lengthened or shortened? We create the one we love but we are creations of others. Parenthetically, we hurt the ones we love (Wilde) more than others. If a passionate love can rapidly turn to hate, how genuine are our emotions? In philosophical debate, realism, I would argue, is obviously false but everyone believes it to be true, while idealism is evidently true but is believed to be false (especially its endpoint in solipsism, which most philosophers would agree is coherent and unassailable but not to be believed). If the logic of a statement or theory is impeccable but the argument is judged to be false, how trustworthy are other logical proofs? Such difficulties can make a philosophy of mind insoluble.

Part of the problem stems from common sense. Common sense is an attitude that arises on a foundation of innate and early-acquired beliefs as an evolutionary coping strategy. A belief in the reality of objects—agency, other minds, cause and effect, etc.—is necessary for survival. In order to perceive the world, the mind has to generate a mirror of reality consistent with physical law; the model generated is an approximation to the real. The creation of a simulacrum is rejected by those who believe in direct perception. Though the imaginary nature of the world is incomprehensible to most people—and is obscured by common sense— it is strongly felt in psychosis.

This psychic model separates two realities, one pointing outward to a noumenal world inferred from the accuracy of perception, and one turning inward to the physical brain and the physiological unconscious (which are also inferences from conscious experience). Indeed, each segment in the mental state must correspond to a comparable process in the brain state. Presumably, the brain follows the same physical laws as those of external reality, while the mind seems to defy many physical laws in order to achieve a veridical image. More precisely, while the representation of the world in consciousness exhibits many features of the same physical laws as the brain state, a paradox arises: an accurate representation of the real is based on or necessitates a variety of illusory phenomena that are essential to mirror reality.

Illusions are essential accessories that approximate mentality to reality. For example, the specious present in which we live, which is essential to consciousness of past and future, is an illusory arch over the instantaneity of physical passage. Dreams are unreal and have no relation to reality, but they reveal a primitive self and consciousness of imagery that are precursors to waking perception. There are no colors in the physical spectrum, but the perception of color, even among lower forms, is necessary for survival. There is no feeling or duration in the acoustic noise of music, yet without duration the perception of a melody, or language, is impossible. Perceptual illusions and object constancies circumvent the physical laws of optics in the service of an adequate representation of the world. These and many other phenomena are necessary for self-identity, agency, awareness and veridical perception. The specificity of individuation of the mental state under constraint by sensation makes possible the precision of scientific demonstration, yet at the same time raises questions as to the nature and boundaries of the phenomenal.

The problem of self-reference owes to the fact that reality can only be inferred from a conceptual model, the accuracy of which is supplemented by methods to overcome the limits of perception. Every scientific fact involves some aspect of mentality as a correlate of the physical unknown. Thus, value, which determines what is observed, is a residua in every fact. Imagination is more important than logic in scientific discovery. Intuition precedes proof in the solution to mathematical (and other) problems. Such attributes of mind are not found in the physical world, and, *sensu stricto,* they do not follow causal law, but are essential to creative advance and ineluctable in its products. Scientific deduction, which attempts to strip away the subjective underpinnings of objective demonstration, is like enjoying a meal oblivious to its ingredients.

∽

If some aspects of experience were physically real and others illusory, we would be confused. The coherence of the mental state requires that all experience is illusory with gradations of realness depending on sensibility.

The most proximate impact of reality is sensation, from which we experience the effects, not the objects or events from which sensations arise. Even were we to experience the physical reality of sensation, it would come to us piecemeal in innumerable impacts, such as light and sound waves, not the physical world behind the sensible.

Among the reflexive phenomena is the fact that the world impacts the self that creates it; that the possibility of multiple selves does not necessitate multiple worlds; that if the self is presumed to be an illusion, who then is it that strives, suffers, enjoys, or fears aging and death?

To deny the self or to claim that perceptual objects are mind-independent, but maintain that consciousness is a fundamental problem for theory of mind, is incoherent since the self is the anchor of a conscious state and objects are its terminus.

The self, objects and mental contents are relational but have a thing-like quality, unlike consciousness which is pure relation.

If you agree there is a feeling of agency, there must be an agent.

Dismissing certain phenomena as illusory is nonsense. All mental phenomena are illusions, some more real than others.

The question is not whether such and such phenomena are illusory but whether they help us to know true facts.

Objects and hallucinations are images "inside" the mind, generated by the brain, but some images are more reliable than others.

If an illusion is a phenomenon that does not actually exist, and if all mental phenomena are illusory, in what sense do we actually exist?

Reflexivity

To postulate a real physical world beyond its illusory representation is also to assume a real physical person beyond an individual mind.

The cogito sought to dispel this doubt. However, all that can be said is that the "I" is part of thought and that thinking is going on.

If this is true, if there is only thinking, we are experiencing an after-life while we are alive.

What is left out in the cogito is feeling, which more than thought is the basis of existence.

Subject, Self, Object

*The self is to the subjectivity of the mind as the
beloved is to the objectivity of the world.*

THE SUBJECT/OBJECT RELATION HAS been a central concern for me over many years. To some extent, the significance of the topic boils down to whether mental phenomena and external objects are interpreted according to a synchronic or diachronic perspective. The position taken on this approach goes to the very heart of a theory of mind. Is an oak effectively the object it appears to be despite moment-to-moment alterations and seasonal variations? Is it the sum of its constituent changes or the category embracing those changes? Does it include its developmental history beginning with an acorn? Are the seedling and the mature oak the same tree? How should we think of the process of change that transforms one instance of the tree into its successor? This problem is similar to that for any object represented in the mind—an oak, a chair—that becomes an independent thing in the world. Does the momentary pre-history of the object figure in its description, or can we ignore prior stages and treat the object as standing alone and independent?

If we eliminate the history and the becoming of the object, that is, the micro-temporal transition that leads to the object, the mind/brain process through which the object is realized goes out the window and the object is conceived as independent of its origin and derivation. In the case of an oak, the growth of the tree seems a uniform and thoroughly external occurrence, a sequence of ostensibly mind-independent events, and this is no doubt true for the tree in extra-psychic reality, as for all physical entities. But the object, the tree in perception, is generated in the mind/brain. The entity in physical reality after which the perception is modeled is presumably also realized over a series of recurrent phases. However, all we know or have immediate knowledge of is the model or representation, not the entity that is modeled. Every object is the outcome of a momentary growth process buried at unconscious strata invisible to the observer, except so far as earlier phases are exposed by experimental and pathological studies.

From such sources, one surmises that objects in perception are the endpoints of a rapid sequence of phases that pass from mind-internal to a locus in the outer world; from a construct in the mind to an image in external space. The formative phases seem to trail the object like the tail of a comet, except that they are imminent in its structure, as conceptual, affective and memorial content. Merleau-Ponty has said, rightly, that an object is remembered into perception; Whitehead had much the same view. The question is how to characterize the transition from a thought- or memory-like experience to a perception-like experience, one internal, the other external, as well as the problem of a sharp cut-off when objects separate, and how subjectivity is for the most part left behind as the image objectifies. The effect of sensibility is to force the detachment of the mental image as a real object that leaves the psyche instead of a transmission of mind into the object itself.

The diachronic process recurs over long and short durations. A long duration would be the maturation of a person over the life span or the growth of an oak over years. A brief duration is the rapid transit of phases in object-perception, and one still briefer is the duration of a particle. This process, which appears longitudinal regardless of duration, is an instantaneous becoming-into-being, or an actualization into completeness, that recurs each moment in the existence of the object or physical entity. How the distinction of inner and outer comes about goes back to the earliest stages in the separation of mind and world.

The distinction of subject and object, then of a self within a subject, begins in the infant, initially with a diffuse subjectivity that is carved into the mind of the baby and within the baby's mind, the image of the mother. This occurs as some portion of subjectivity objectifies as the breast or nourishing object. This object, usually the mother, is perceived as close to or part of the infant's body, a partition of its mental space. At first, there is no definite subject-object relation; rather, a parcel of the infant's perceptual field consolidates in a proximate image of the mother or surrogate. Gradually, the maternal image separates as a relatively independent object, while the interior of the infant's mind specifies a variety of fleeting contents—images, dreams, feelings. Over time a subjective node early in object-formation forms a core self within the subjective field. Concurrently, the extrinsic portion of the infant's mental space, occupied by the maternal presence, undergoes partition to a myriad of objects that articulate the perceptual landscape. Still for the infant, the outer world is an objectified portion of a subjective space that only gradually becomes fully external.

In the transition from inner to outer, value is the umbilicus that ties the detachment of the world to its birthplace in the observer's mind, with sensibility the knife that cuts the cord of feeling that binds the observer to objects of his own making. There is no addition of elements; rather, an individuation within a whole—in human mind, the subjective field—with one set of constituents clearly psychic, and another, also subjective, felt as external. The continuation of the mitotic pattern of unpacking from within, analogous to the splitting of cells within a membrane, occurs in a bubble of subjectivity, the psychic space helmet in which we live, as the field individuates to populate the inner and outer segments of a single sheet of mentation.

∽

We do not attach feeling to external objects. The feeling is a sign of the value that stretches from drive and desire to the objectified image.

We sense a continuity of feeling when we care for others, even things that are inanimate.

The tree sounds and still falls in the forest unobserved, but perceiving the tree makes a difference. The former is reality-inferred, the latter, reality-mediated.

Coalescence of a self occurs in the partition of drive to desire.

Like a fragile skiff on a mighty sea, the self, if not heroically reasserted, is easily drowned.

The self seeks pleasure in the value of the objects it creates

The many selves I have been are branches of the one self that I am.

Value survives the parsing of sensibility since feeling is resistant to adaptive sculpting.

The concept contains the affect that distributes into the object.

An object is an exemplar of a concept, or category. What remains in the concept is implicit in the object.

The object is isolated by value inherited from the concept.

When feeling is withdrawn from an object of interest, it returns to a uniform multiplicity.

An hallucination is an image that approximates an object as it bursts through sensibility.

The not fully external is a clue to the mental origin of the external, in its dream-like space and meaning-content.

Superficial contents such as images are more likely to externalize than those closer to drive and the self.

The self that precipitates early in mind can dissolve into background subjectivity, on and off, day and night, but most emphatic in meditation.

In becoming the self of the next moment, the prior self is forgotten. The self cannot be recalled like an object or idea apart from events perceived. The self remembers but is not itself a memory.

The self that is valued above all is an agent or source of valuation, not a repository.

As a condensation of the subjective and a foundational category, the self can escape opposition to its imagery in dreamless sleep, meditation and unreflective spontaneous acts.

To seek the genuine self is futile. To wish to be free of one's self is the beginning of wisdom.

Like a geyser that bubbles up, the self is an intermittent eruption in homogeneity.

Concepts and categories

*In the flux of object change, constancy in a
category overrides vicissitudes*

WE THINK IN OPPOSITIONS—BLACK/WHITE, right/wrong, night/day—with polarities arbitrary and distinctions gradients. The intra-psychic transition of self to others consolidates opposing entities at poles in a spectrum, pure inventions, like the opposition of hot and cold. The continuity from subject to object in mind becomes a confrontation with others at the interface of self and world. Every object can be a sole category or a member of a larger one. A tree is a member of an infinite family of past and present trees, shrubs and bushes, but it is also a category of a specific tree, which preserves its identity over momentary, seasonal and longer durations.

Categories preserve identity over successive states. The category of dogs, or of a particular dog arches over multiple occurrences in its momentary existence. Language decants concepts into containers, selecting one thing among many and freezing it in a name. To name a chair strips it of conceptual richness and the potential for other objects. In writing, revision attempts to find a certain resonance just waiting to be uncovered. Words and objects invite propagation but they also narrow possibility. A thing once labeled loses its force. A dynamic solidifies in an object, leaving a concept that could still generate a multiplicity of other objects. A concept as an object is static, as a category it is inexhaustible. Thousands of pages and a world of objects can be generated from a single idea, even a single word, while potential stagnates in denotation.

As a category, the organism is a compilation of multiple instances of itself, of changes in behavior and appearance over time, a composite of tenderness and anger, concern or uncaring, affection or dispassion, a

Concepts and categories

repository of states with unchanging identity. The love of a pet (a dog or a parakeet) with an anthropocentric reading of instinct as love, loyalty or devotion, is intermediate in the valuation of animate and inanimate objects depending on the cognitive status of the organism.

An idealized pet, parent, child, car, home or diamond, can take precedence over a beloved as surrogate fulfillment with little reciprocity. This is nothing to sneeze at. The intensity of loving in proportion to reciprocity makes love conditional. Yet, as the sole member of a singular category, the beloved, an ideal of wonder and an embodiment of longing, is truly a work of art, a creation of the imagination, indeed a finished work of art, not a struggle with incessant revision, though both lover and beloved are changing, for what love creates must be continuously renewed. The truth is that a love that endures recurs, and the constancy of recurrence in the face of variability, in self and other, is protected by the categorical nature of identity.

For many, particulars are the real things of the world, but the passage from category, as potential, to part as a potential (category) for further specification implies that the particular is a resting point in possible further partitions. For example, an individual can be conceived as a solid object independent of mind or as a multitude of constituent tissues, a manifold of moods, mental states, aging, sickness and health. The objectified particular is a momentary focus or snapshot of a categorical potential for further analysis.

The tree that blossoms in summer is the same tree that is barren and bent with ice in winter. The set of features, if sufficiently plastic, constitute defining properties for the identity of objects, though the features of category-belongingness are too general to define individuals. Birds have two legs, wings and feathers, but that does not distinguish one type or instance of a bird from another. Featherless biped does not distinguish one person from another.

From a subjective standpoint, acts, words and objects represent an arbitrary arrest of a whole/part process, passing from the widest frame, such as organic/inorganic, through successive partitions to microphysical entities such as elementary particles or superstrings. The particularities of mind condense at a macro-level intermediate between the infinitesimal and the universal, between the immensity of time and space and the locality of a moment. Categories develop to actualities from the widest, most inclusive, to the narrowest or most individual.

We are each irreplaceable though we all are redundant
Sameness is approximation to likeness in a category
Are mice identical with the same DNA?
Not even an identical twin is identical to himself
How can you know anything if a thing includes what it is not? Objects are contrasts defined by what they exclude.
Do not tell me who you are, tell me what you are not
Every act dies the moment it is born, though its consequences live on
Lack of decisiveness is the breeding ground of conscience
Reason provides the rationale for actions already decided
Before an act, reasons are justifications; after, they are excuses
Justice cannot avoid loyalty. There is bias in every act of thought
Steer your craft between fate and fortune
The secret of the flower is the riddle of the universe.
The leaf that freely quivers in the breeze is still tethered to the root.
Confidence comes to those who forget how little they know
Educated beyond his capacity he had a fact for every occasion but no occasion for any fact.

How do we understand spontaneous categories, such as things needed to camp in the desert? How does a superordinate category provide a novel occasion to elicit diverse members?

My routine in the morning is not a natural category like animals or trees. The category is a limit on what it calls up, but it can be called up by what it includes.

The scientific concept of a class reflects category-formation in mind that goes back to hunter-gatherers and beyond.

Animals form novel categories, such as a ruse to catch a prey, or unusual things to eat in a time of scarcity.

Particulars are ingredients of experience that differ from "bloodless" categories in the feeling of realness.

A particular arrests a category-derivation, but every particular is a category of implicit parts.

Life parses the improbable to the necessary.

Necessity may be the mother of invention but imagination is the mistress of originality

Reality is the totality of particulars apart from the world image in which they are perceived.

A rock pile is an aggregate in the world and a category in the mind.

Were there no categories, the world would come to us piecemeal.

The contrasts that divide up the world are the origins of the concepts that navigate it.

Primitive concepts are necessary to attend to one thing instead of another.

The phenomenal quality of duration applies to all categories. Every object is an event-category that is arbitrarily bounded.

Change, Replication and Process

*The stability of the world is carved out of change;
events are bounded in flux so objects can be isolated*

WHAT COULD BE MORE fundamental and perplexing than the nature of change, and that of time to which it is linked? Some have argued that time is continuous; most believe it is instantaneous and that change is causal, namely, a succession of instants. This is a controversy that goes back thousands of years to Zeno, and to the arguments of Heraclitus and Parmenides, brilliantly captured in a painting by Magritte.

This way of thinking appeals to common sense. We have a powerful feeling of forward movement over time in concert with aging, and with change in the surrounding world. This forward motion—the measure of time for Aristotle—is presumed to be a causal succession. While causation cannot specify how the cause is carried into the effect, or what happens in the causal shift, or how and at what point change occurs, it remains the dominant theory of change, in science and in everyday thought. In contrast, for the idea of incessant recurrence, which is a kind of facsimile theory akin to those in Asian and process philosophies, the challenge is in ascribing change to inexactness. Otherwise, nature would be frozen, like a frame in a movie reel that sequentially comes into view.

My way of thinking comes from the study of human mind and brain, and a theory of the mental state, in which all entities self-replicate each moment and change is recurrent not progressive. In other words, the change in "causal progression" is not forward motion but inexact replication. The mental state generates the present as a point that does not move. Bergson wrote that we spatialize time when we think of it as a two-dimensional line. Instead, the point recurs, with change interpreted as movement to a future that does not exist until another present is created. In a mind-independent world, there is only before and after. Each instantiation of the mental state is part of a universe that also recurs. All things—organic and inorganic—recur each moment. Existence is predicated on a becoming-into-being as entities recur to become what they are.

Some inorganic entities have autogenic replication. Some organisms have parthenogenesis, most replicate in mating. These are recognized by everyone, but the replication of each entity is less obvious. Mind recurs each moment, as does the world it elaborates, and in which it is embedded. In all cases, recurrence is the theme. The grand cycles of life, birth and death, night and day, seasonal rotation, the orbits of celestial bodies, electrons, the vibrations of superstrings, all come down to recurrence, with linear time and causal progression a result of seamless replacement. Things recur with subtle change each moment to give the impression of forward motion. In this process, energy takes on direction as feeling empowers existence.

In overlapping waves, the mental state develops from unconscious core to conscious surface in a fraction of a second, a transition in physical time of before and after or earlier and later. In a sequence of states, the overlap revives the prior state with less complete revival over the series. The degree of revival of a past state within the present is termed decay or forgetting, with degrees of completeness that determine if it is immediate, short or long term. However, a failure of revival is not a sign of decay, which implies the degrading of a persistent trace. Incomplete revival is the key to understanding subjective time and the present. The embedding in the present of prior revivals descends to a "floor" in the mental state beyond which revival is not possible. The disparity of the floor of the state to the perceptual surface is extracted as the duration of the present moment. This duration is elaborated as a recurrent point—the illusory bubble of the now—with the self coextensive with the floor. Earlier to later provides the substrate of past and future as opposing sides in the present. That is, in the creation of the now, the physical time of before and after becomes the subjective time of past, present and future.

The slow transformation in an organism is invisible, replacing each moment as entities are revived. A satisfactory renewal leads to growth and the appearance of stability; an incomplete or altered renewal is decay or decline. A thing persists over time when recurrence is similar, but each recurrence is a change in growth, an advance or deterioration. Nothing persists. Covert replacement is the source of object stability. An organism keeps growing into itself until replacement runs its course. Early phases embedded in the next state preserve the identity of the core self and experiential memory, while later phases perish so the world can be renewed. Inexactness is the reciprocal of stability and the basis for growth; the before replaced by the after, the earlier by the later, with novelty in passage the signature of growth. The perishability of structure is overcome by replacement.

Prior causes do not exist at the moment of the present effect, while in mind the present embodies and emerges from the past. In causal theory, the open-ended progression of sustained growth would leave bypassed phases vulnerable to absolute forgetting. Can stability be explained on a causal basis? Does an entity, an organism, cause itself to recur (causal persistence)? If each causal step reproduces a new entity, how does this explain growth, what would guarantee identity, what propels causation and what is the nature of change?

The deep memory of inorganic matter is atomic structure in constant flux.

Dissolution is not cessation of growth but failure to achieve renewal. Death ensues when organs are irreparable. Decline is an exhaustion of renewal; it is not a simple decay of structure or functional arrest.

༄

A not-nothing before it is something takes on motion and direction

The cause or the effect is non-existent when either the cause or the effect is present

The passage from potential to actual is from possibility to commitment; that from cause to effect is from one conceptual entity to another

The difficulty to describe potential is no greater than to describe cause. The boundaries of the cause must be demarcated; the content of potential must be ascertained

The present is a fiction but as real as it gets

The illusory present arches over passage as a point, a perspective, a center of existence

Billions of human lives, not brains or bodies but perspectives reinstated

One does not move to the future, the next moment replaces the last

There is no chain of instants, but overlapping pulsations that inherit the past

If we are near-facsimiles of what came before

Something of the first is preserved in the last

A past revived but never repeated, repeated but never revived.

I am a replica each moment of the moment just before

Change, Replication and Process

What begins as replication, continues as recurrence
From the prion to the flower, self-replication is the key.
If all things are contrasts, how can there be unity
Difference is relatedness. Even in identity there is contrast
Is it not remarkable that we are all different yet composed of the same elements?
Is energy conserved in wholes or aggregates?
Microgenesis is a fractal theory but the partitions are dissimilar
The rapture of love is forecast in the dance of the honeybee
The wonder of nature is that even the inanimate is alive
Things recur with subtle change each moment to give the impression of forward motion
Time is not a river but a fountain, with objects the froth at the surface
The gap between the phenomenal and the noumenal is misconstrued. All experience of the physical comes of the adaptation of mind to external conditions..
The constraints of the brain on the actualization of the mental are like those of sensibility on perception.
The supposed gap to reality is a continuum of approximations.
Reason can help to decide only if one option is irrational; and not even then.

> If decision is motivated by belief or emotion, what is the role of thought?

One distinction of mind from automata is the irrational and the creative, the other is feeling.
Is action a continuation of thought, its implementation or an alternate mental state?
In a dream, I thought these lines:[1]
"Run thee a poem in your time
Pay not a fare to the rhyme or the meter"
A dream in which docket and pocket money rhymed convinced me the neocortical areas, especially the Wernicke area, is active in dream.
We let go of the past to become someone new, but without the past there is no someone to whom newness can occur.

---

1. Run a poem = write a great work, live a life. In your time = of your life, the poem. Pay not a fare = neglect the meter of life, disregard the rhyme.

Reflections on Mind and the Image of Reality

Process that decants to a single pattern from which all is created is another name for god.

The cycles of change in nature return the actual to the potential of their origin.

☙

The cypress sways in the wind
But the clouds are motionless.
The eternity of heaven smiles
On our paltry strivings below

Caught up in momentary change
We do not feel the planetary spin
The measure of day and night
That passes in silent uniformity

What exists is what becomes
From core to destination
Wholes are not collected sums
But process and relation

Motion is in everything
In whole and in the parts
Each concrete thing is perishing,
Before the last one starts

What comes and goes comes again
From long forgot enclaves
Seamlessly the new refrain
Blankets doubled waves

Between moments

That for which we are unaware makes awareness possible.

The temporal gap between moments, obvious in causal theory, implies an infinite regress of instants like incremental motion in a paradox of Zeno. Between moments, timelessness is non-existence or an alternate time, an absence, a ghostly presence, an aura encircling the now, a death that separates living moments, girds and surrounds them. Were I to surrender an encapsulated sequence of moments for an alternate series, what possible lives could be lived adjacent to the dominant mode of experience, what worlds, real or imaginary, lived or unlived, familiar or unfamiliar, lie hidden in the cracks of perception, shadows of the deepest night outside the perimeter of my viewpoint, occluded by a consciousness that opens one door as it closes another?

We think of life as linear, and time as a motion from before to after. The stream continues; moments surge, drops of experience in the swells of a bottomless sea, each droplet, each "I am that I am" in the midst of the all, the nothingness, an illusory interlude of self-realization, a breath that sustains, revives, perseveres against the breathless, the emptiness, the timelessness about a life unfelt between moments, relishing the before, postponing the after, the voracious predator of living time that, when it expires, devours the oncoming now and you—there is no you , only an absence—dissolved in the fabric of succession, unknown voices wailing in endless recurrence, the moment eternal, the life overlapping, subsiding, finally, for the unattended companion who has been waiting all along.

∽

There is no awareness for an isolated moment. Consciousness needs a series.

If we each generate a personal subjective time, a slight discrepancy in inter-subjective time judgment is possible.

Does the span of illusory duration keep us in synch with others?

Better nothing between moments than an infestation of alternate selves.

Is the nothing that receives us at the final now a something or a not-nothing that is not yet a something?

Those who fear that respiration will cease if they are not conscious of breathing have a glimpse of the struggle for existence every fraction of a second.

I spent some hours in Sikkim with a Buddhist monk discussing what happens between moments. The monk was puzzled by the question, but what happens between moments is critical, and a deeper problem than the nature of the moment itself.

Every presence is limited by an absence: the space between objects, the silence between sounds.

Buddhism postulates a causal chain of moments (ksana), but how do they arise?

The duration of a moment cannot be measured in clock time. For one thing, there are no increments.

Since a moment cannot endure if everything is in flux, duration must be illusory.

The seamless transition between moments could be due to the rapidity of change, or to the memory of antecedents or to the overlap of consequents. Or, the illusory might transcend the in-between to obscure physical gaps.

Say it takes 10 mental states to generate consciousness. The Buddhists claim over 50. Why then do I feel consciousness as continuous?

If what is carried over is from the antecedent state, and what is conveyed to that state is from its antecedent, are we not a cumulative history rather than an outcome?

Like rings on an oak, every mental state incorporates the life-history of the person.

Is a person the sum of all states or the final state? If the final state, what do prior acts count for?

Judgment is a pragmatic assessment that ignores the phenomenal nature of content.

I am not exactly the same person I was a moment ago. Judgment is for a category of innumerable states of self.

Between moments

Clarence Darrow gave a sound argument, but to accept it is to forego responsibility. I should be held responsible even for acts I do not remember.

Is it unreasonable to hold responsible the children of criminals? Certainly, they should feel guilt and act in a way to merit the repentance their parents rejected.

Those who believe in transmigration might hold someone responsible for acts in a prior life.

If no man is an island, no family is without guilt.

> All things perish to exist
> Die in time to timeless be
> Nothing can in time persist
> Without a brief eternity
>
> The living present does not stay
> Gives way to its recurrence
> A present past, a brief delay
> The real is not existence
>
> If before and if to follow
> As events do not exist,
> Present time for all we know
> Must unreal be to persist
>
> Things within an instant change
> Yet still remain the same
> One the other does exchange
> Which then the wholes reclaim

Experience

The mind, not the world, is the starting point of experience

THE COMMON WAY OF thinking about experience is that it is the sum of sensory input, or sensory impingement on the brain: some of which is unconscious background, some of which is a focus of attention. All or some portion of sensibility that enters the brain is relayed to memorial content and adds to the knowledge base. There are also effects on the body itself which may or may not register in the brain or in consciousness. This approach assumes that the sensory world encountered each moment is ingredient in cognition and evokes prior experience to produce meaningful ideas or objects.

One problem with this perspective is that, if acts of cognition begin with sensibility, we would be unable to decide what to look at, what to do, or how to feel, until provoked by external stimuli. This leads me to wonder how sensibility undergoes unification, or becomes experience, or how it is organized as knowledge, that is, the unity of conscious experience. This reactive theory of mind requires a combinatorial assemblage of externally delivered "information" from which mind and world are constructed before action in that world can occur.

A preferred way of thinking is that the mind/brain state develops and re-creates the world each moment out of memorial or experiential data constrained by sensation at multiple phases. This is a generative process that begins in infants who have an innate rudimentary "model" of the world, which is progressively carved out by sensation to a more adequate representation of reality. Individuals create a world of their own making, in which sensibility provides a private window on the external. Shared sensibility also provides a common ground for different minds, while differences relate to the vagaries of individual experience. A person is not a receptor but an agent of occasions and events; this is a self-realization that, for some, is strongly exercised, for others weakly felt. Even in infants, strong motor tone and grasping predict a more outgoing personality. Granting accidents of life and the contingencies of encounters, degrees of purposefulness elaborate a mirror image of the world in which the individual lives.

There is reason to believe that the incidental or unattended may have a more profound impact on thought and perception than what is consciously experienced. The least noticed fragments of daytime experience tend to recur as the epicenter of dream content. The incidental does not reach a conscious endpoint, but corresponds with antecedent phases in conscious perception. That is, in perception, preliminary phases recur as traces of experience that are replaced and/or lost at the conscious surface. In the replacement of mental states, the preliminary survive while the distal perish. On occasion, there is vivid near-veridical clarity of recollected events, but more often recall has a vague, even affective, quality in which past experience is felt more than remembered. Kierkegaard summed up his life as a red mood.

Even the most intense experience tends to fade to the unconscious, with an influence on thought and behavior that may not become conscious. The incompleteness of recurrence coincides with that of the unnoticed, such that dream arouses formative phases in the mental state: those which are incompletely revived, and those that are part of the ambient environment. The incidental, embedded in the structure of the perception, concurrent with conscious events that have faded, comprises the bedrock of experience, the foundation of the self and the mental state from which, parsed by sensation, a viable model of the world actualizes.

This is not to say that experience is independent of sensibility; rather, that it is shaped by the mental state in accordance with individual need, knowledge, interest and desire. The experience we have, and what we make of it—a daily commute to a monotonous job or an expedition to the Amazon—is determined by needs and interests in each momentary slice of perception. Consider a tree that appears before me as an occasion of experience. The tree actualizes out of the mind as antecedent phases are constrained by sensation to realize an external image. To a botanist, the tree is a specimen, to an aesthete, a thing of beauty, to others, shade, shelter or firewood. This does not reflect an initial perception that is associated to experience, but the experiential, memorial and contextual ground out of which the tree and its personal meaning are perceived.

Reflections on Mind and the Image of Reality

Whether sensibility builds up experience or constrains it, some fraction of a second transpires before the experience is conscious

Those who seek travel and adventure are like collectors who save up books or stamps. For one, memories are possessions, for the other, things.

Some live in the past, others for the future, but all experience, inner and outer, is in the present.

To live in the present is commendable even if it is impossible

We do not call on experience. Experience awakens and calls on us.

Perceptions create experience but we create perceptions

How should we enjoy an experience if its enduring effect is non-conscious?

Since experience begins in the mind, why look elsewhere? Ruskin thought a guide book and an armchair were enough in a person of imagination.

I have traveled widely but friends insist that I see the Galapagos before I die. Yet, I can read Darwin and enjoy it more, or Conrad on the Congo, Wordsworth on the Alps, and so on.

Nearing 80, I have no desire to store up experience, just a need to understand it better

On this note, I would like to really understand just one thing

For some, the evening sky is wondrous and romantic, for others, the realm of the divine, paradise, a vast terrifying emptiness, astrological symbols, maps, directions, clumps of gas or matter; for Hegel, the stars were a rash on the sky. Stripped of mentality, it is what? Can we know anything stripped of mentality?

To gaze at Machu Picchu for a few minutes, take a mental photograph and go home. To what end?

Tom Nagel wrote of the view from outside. It is difficult to sustain this perspective, not only because it is depressing but because the objective point of view is a subjective experience.

By the way, I fail to understand the subjectivity of a bat, not because I am not a bat, or a particular bat, but because I do not believe a bat has a "what it's like to be" experience.

For the Buddhists, experience is cumulative to the last breath. Is this additive history of a life the person at the final moment?

If I am what I have become, does it matter what I have been? If all that survives is what I am now, what happened to the person I was then?

If something I have done is forgotten, and erased from my brain, in what sense am I responsible?

If I am punished for something that has been totally obliterated from my brain, it would seem I am not the guilty person.

Redemption is to be applauded but it points to a sense of guilt.

Perception records experience in memory, but memory creates the perception that accounts for experience.

My friend, Karl Pribram came to New York to prepare for a trip to the jungle. I get that!

I remember people or conversations more than sights, but mostly the women along the way.

If I am the sum of my experience, do I add to that sum each moment, or exchange one experience for another? Do similar experiences cancel each other out?

Though an experience is unconscious, or cannot be retrieved, does it vanish completely or is there a picture-strip of everything as some have maintained?

Warren McCullough found total recall in hypnosis. In trance, the return to earlier phases accesses memories below the conscious threshold.

Experience is not stored as a picture in a mental archive but consists in the relative strengths of myriad synapses in stratified, distributed patterns or configurations. If experience can be revived by a fragment, an odor, a face, a photograph, it is not because each neuron, as in holographic theory, can reconstruct the whole; rather, the fragment activates some portion of the configuration which then arouses the pattern. I meet an old friend after many years but have forgotten his face. A few words and it all comes back. This is to be expected if events are categories that can be emptied by the recollection of one detail.

Oliver Sacks, who achieved celebrity for eccentricity, unexceptional writing and chronic Eureka experiences, did make one clever remark, though he failed to note its significance. He once said in response to an interrogation, I know it but don't remember it. Most of what we know we don't remember, when or where it was learned. I know that ice is cold, the meanings of words, the laws of geometry, but when did I first experience these phenomena? I know that zebras have stripes but experience tells me there might be albino zebras.

Experiences may be ordered in memory—stacked or serialized—but the inability to recall all or any experience implies a melting and possible erasure of like occasions, perhaps due to shared or similar configural patterns, while only exemplary instances stand out. If I take a train to work each day, I cannot recall each specific trip unless something unusual occurs. I have seen many rickshaws and visited many palaces and temples in India, but they all dissolve to the knowledge of Indian rickshaws and palaces, not a particular experience. In the same way, a similar trip on a train occludes or replaces others as individual episodes dissolve in the category of the commutation. How does a unique and passing experience, perhaps noticing an attractive stranger, facilitate recall of that episode when otherwise it would be forgotten?

If an event in the world is much the same each day—an alarm clock, the arrival of a train—we do not say the events are habits. The habitual is waking each day at a certain hour or taking the same train. Habitual experience points to actions of the agent, not external events. Regularity applies to the external, to the cycle of day and night or the seasons, but habit refers to recurrent behavior. To the extent an event departs from regularity it is perceived as a novel experience. The more things change in a person's world, the more varied the experience. Conversely, the regularity of events reinforces the idea of experience as internally-determined. While the replication of the mental state each moment repeats the cycles of material law, experience consists of categories of change that bridge replications. Here, at the boundary of mind and world, we see more closely how mind drives experience. Even with random events or accidents, the individual engages activities that determine the momentary occasion.

The retention of the past in the present means that the world has moved on even as it is perceived.

Experience in the present is inevitably in the past. What you experience now is what you experienced then. The only difference is the distance from the immediate future.

The scope of experience narrows in aging as its depth increases.

Wisdom is in knowing more than you can say. Foolishness is saying more than you know.

The lack of novel experience comes of a lessening of interest, not lack of novelty.

Intelligence is the ability to solve problems; wisdom is in knowing which problems to solve.

Experience

We might agree there are multiple modes of intelligence, but does this not show that learning is guided by a difference of interest, that is, from within?

To see how knowledge could be constructed from sensibility is more difficult than to know how it reinforces intentionality.

In action, knowledge is skill. What is the relation of knowledge as skill to knowledge as intelligence?

In frontal brain injury, the dissociation of knowing what to do and doing it confirms that knowledge can forecast but is not a causal precursor.

The difference between the prodigy and the autistic savant comes down to novelty in repetition and an expansion of skill to thought.

The pleasure in living a full life depends on vivid remembrance and a retrospective gaze.

Dive in life, feel the bliss
Or life itself is what you'll miss

Like sheep grazing on fresh grass, limited time and dearth of recollection prompt the elderly to seek new experience.

Adventure becomes tourism when an occasion is digested, not lived.

Photography destroys the moment in attempting to preserve it.

The simpleton seeks to be wise but the wise seek simplicity.

>Things arise from unknown wells
>Unfathomed in descent
>To end as fragmentary shells
>Sculpted in ascent
>
>Is the core from nature sifted
>Or within the mind
>Is the human psyche gifted
>In degree or kind
>
>If the ground's an Absolute
>Rock-solid or relation
>Are there any so astute
>To narrow speculation

Meaning in life

Meaning points to something beyond what is said. What this something is, is the question.

THE MEANING THAT MANY are seeking is not in the world waiting to be encountered. It is uncovered and cultivated in ourselves when we settle on the path we have chosen. Even then, it is not the path itself but what we create along the way that provides the will to persevere. For most, great hopes and expectations early in life fall away like tattered clothes as the dreary chores of life, work and family are imbued with a larger, even impersonal, meaning from which sustenance is gathered. Yet when all is done, we look back and realize that life and work matter little, even less in the tide of human history and an indifferent cosmos, so all that remains for most to give meaning to a meaningless life is the family left behind. Those who accomplish little find meaning in progeny, friendships and small pleasures, relishing petty satisfactions; those who accomplish much will, even with pride, regret their failures more than their successes.

Suppose we say one should live according to the belief that life is without purpose other than to fulfill the bestial impulse for which we are designed? Even so, we would serve nature in accomplishment, which is not meant as a gift but as a magnet for power, prestige, money, thus status and/or sexual partners. Is it possible to accept that everything we do is meaningless, yet still have a satisfying life without fear or melancholy? The search for some quota of meaning in the objectively meaningless comes from the nature of our brains as engines of meaning-creation. That is, meaning and purpose are essential in category-formation, since members—words, objects—are bound by meaning-relations. Meaning and purpose specify out of these relations, which are virtual until they actualize. Meaning accompanies the developing object in the outward thrust of process. This forward-realization, the direction to the future, the externalization and exportation of words and objects, the specification out of generality, the feeling or value within the actualization process, a self antecedent to the particulars of conscious experience, all give focus and purpose to the act, qualities not applied from without but ingredient in the becoming.

Meaning is bound up with experience and memory. When we have an experience, we tend to give meaning even to random events, and call it fate, destiny, payback, hope for salvation, god testing us and so on. The mind/brain state cannot adequately absorb an event without embedding it in a narrative relating to the life story. This is accentuated when the event is remembered, in the re-working that occurs in revival. Naturally, there will be events that fall outside the sphere of meaning—a brick falling on one's head—but such events are then integrated with other experiences and take on meaning in relation to their role in future life.

This is a striking feature of dreams, in which the effort to assign meaning to seemingly disparate or random phenomena reflects less the meaningfulness of the phenomena than the urge to interpretation, to find meaning in all experience. Dream events can be construed as divinations, adaptations, consolidations of memory, symbolic representations and so on. The search for a function is also a search for meaning, since we do not accept that events occur without reason—as causes or effects—and the reason why an event occurs is an aspect of its meaning, whether a dream, a perception or the explanation of a physical occurrence such as a bolt of lightning.

Meaning is carried into the becoming of a thing. Once the thing becomes what it is, only then, as it is entrained in subsequent acts of becoming, can it take on meaning. The becoming or subjective aim gives purpose to actuality while its issuance out of category (context), is a passage from the virtual to the real. The appearance of objects in perception is explained by reconstruction of the "out there", but words, thoughts, memories are like miracles in that they seem to arise out of the nothing for which the unconscious is a label. This sense of a bottomless absence from which mental content emerges points to the virtual and non-temporal nature of unactualized categories.

∾

The subjectivity of the world, its origin in mind, is manifest in the meaning attributed to external events.

For mind and world, science strips objects of meaning to examine them as naked facts.

Truth and reason are meta-psychological adjuvants, inert in process, appearing when knowledge, need and value confront sensibility.

Meaning raised a protest as the uninvited guest at the wedding of syntax and computation.

The absence of meaning in music comes as a surprise to those who find it meaningful

I can meditate on death but a Schubert adagio takes me to heaven. Was his sense of mortality a pre-sentiment or a heightened sensitivity?

Are we not dealing with meaning as semantics and meaning as experiential feeling?

The meanings of words impact communication, the meaning in experience affects our life.

Experiential memory, or signification, is the quiet companion of language, a web of memory evoked in speech and perception.

What we mean to say is more elusive than what words convey.

Linguistics, an island of grammar in a sea of knowledge

Language is essential to thought, but this does not mean thought can be described in terms of language.

A formal theory of language is useful, but how does it relate to the psychology of language, or thinking, memory and meaning?

Experiential meaning is more than feeling. It recurs in dream when words have been forgotten or transformed. It stands behind language as an ineffable ground that is diced up in words.

Emotional speech has a greater effect than relaxed discourse. Feeling in words rises with affective tone and lowers with concepts

If someone says, I love you, the natural reaction is, do you mean it? Along with other deceptions, this shows that meaning is anterior to words

In fact, if someone says, I really mean it, we have further cause to doubt

What is meant by the meaning of existence? To exist is to be. To mean is to refer to something extrinsic to being.

The elicitation of meaning in consciousness is an act that is distinct from what the meaning is about.

The meaning in denotation or reference is extracted from connotation or experience in the same way that objects develop out of categories

Experiential meaning includes the implicit relations evoked in metaphor that are explicit in poetry or dream. This constitutes some of the potential in a category.

The politician said, I mean what I say and I say what I mean. Are these the same or different meanings? In both instances, meaning is claimed to motivate speech. The statement is an assertion, not a truth, but the authenticity that is implied cannot be asserted.

To intend to do something differs from asking why you are doing it.

If we ask why we intend to do something, we are asking for the meaning of what is to be done. This begs the question of the nature of an intention.

Ordinarily, we do not intend to carry out a meaningless act. If valuation is for acts that are meaningful, what is the relation of intentionality to meaning?

It can take many words to unpack the meaning in an idea, but sometimes only a few will do. This can depend on the skill of the writer or the work of the reader

The cynic does not believe you mean what you say, or perceives an alternate motivation. Either way, it can end in a state of perpetual doubt that carries distrust to an extreme.

Meaning as the relation of category to content runs parallel to the path of intentionality from self to object.

We do not attach meaning to an object; we reach back into its richness prior to individuation.

Meaning is the residual context of experience after it is reduced to a definition.

Categories are fundamental in mind. Meaning is a secondary outcome of the elicitation of parts from wholes.

Apart from reference, which terminates specification, meaning is often vague. This uncertainty makes us say that something is meaningful.

Thought and memory

Thought is productive memory and memory is reproductive thought

EXCEPT FOR PHOTOGRAPHIC PRODIGIES or rote memorization, memory is rarely exact. If I recall dinner with a friend and I elaborate on our conversation, memory seems to be the starting point for thought. If I think of a particular topic and then recall a related conversation, it is thought that prompts a memory. If I have a thought but do not recall having it before, or I remember a thought, or thought and memory are mixed together in dream or imagination, what is the nature of thought and memory? What happens when a new piece of music is studied, or a medical procedure is learned and gradually becomes habitual (memorial)? Or the reverse, reflection on the over-learned, automatic or habitual? I would say that conscious recall is only possible with the possibility of thought. In both instances there is consciousness of mental content, in all likelihood evolving as a unit.

The accuracy of automatic memory or unconscious learning—that in animals and man is essential to survival—is the foundation of thinking. It is found in the play of verbal and visual imagery, even as thought departs from habit and automaticity. Thought deviates from memory when it is enlivened by metaphor, analogy or similar processes, and propagates over categories. We often attribute the shift from memory to thought as the effect of association, which is merely an extension of causal thinking to mind. I would claim there is no actual association of ideas, nor of brain processes underlying them. Rather, ideas are evoked by the overlap in attributes or expansion of categories to include related members.

If I remember discussing a film with a friend and think about other similar films, or generate ideas based on the film or our conversation, what appears as an association is the revival of experiential memory in categories that overlap based on shared features. When memory provokes reflection, related categories are joined, generally by a single property in common. The outcome is sufficiently distant from experiential memory as to give rise to novel concepts or images.

The problem with association is that items which appear connected in the mind are taken to be the mirror of connections in the brain. That is, there is an inferred correspondence of an association of ideas to associations in brain activity. The sequential nature of ideas or events is the basis of the causal linkage. My coffee and spoon co-occur, spatially, but they are not associated in the world, only in memory or perception. The habit and mere contiguity suggest association, and the absence of the spoon does nothing to contradict this concept. Yet, to conceive them as associations is to say the category of foods or drinks overlaps or expands to include utensils.

The central point of this discussion, and all my writings, is that mind consists of a single process of whole-to-part or category-to-member transition that partitions over phases in the mind/brain state. The process arises in the core of the state and terminates, in wakefulness, in the perception of an external world. The partition occurs in a fraction of a second, distributing into various aspects of cognition. There are no modules dedicated, *ab origine*, to thought, memory, language or emotion, though brain formations become committed over time to certain recurrences in activity.

Forgetting is essential to remembering. Otherwise, we would remember everything when we try to remember anything. What we forget is part of who we are, and what we remember is the outcome of what has not become structure. Involuntary memory is constantly being revived, beginning, say, when we wake up in the morning and the self of yesterday returns, as do habits and everyday conversations. Within this more or less automatic recurrence, we now and then have a memory, or the memory is forced upon us. In dreams, creativity and pathology, memory veers from expectation and automaticity.

Memory, as a transformation of structure, is the outward sign of growth. One can say, the structure of the brain is like the deep waters of an ocean on which the waves of remembrance come and go. Like waters that turn to ice, the structure of the brain, which is as dynamic as an ocean, is artificially frozen into morphology, giving a static or substantial account in which process is a function of structure. However, structure is an ongoing form of behavior, altered by learning, which becomes part of it. Memory takes the form of behavior when structure is conceived as four-dimensional change. The pattern of fetal growth continues throughout life as the microgenetic process of thought and perception. That is, the same process that lays down structure in fetal and postnatal life transmutes to an analogous process that deposits an act of cognition, a mind/brain state. The development of morphology is early behavior; behavior entails growth. Process generates form as structure early in life and then generates form as behavior, with memory a residue of change, and process the medium through which growth and function occur.

In moments of intense concentration, I feared a descent so deep I would not return, yet at such times, precious insights came upon me. Delving into memory, I wanted to go still deeper, to the bottomless, the underpinnings of mind. Timorous, I turned away, my nerves unsteady, guarding my sanity, but forsaking knowledge waiting like buried treasure for those less fearful.

∞

If it means anything at all, "*I think, therefore I am*" means thought exists, and that the thought that I exist embodies the self in thought

Type an x, then delete it. When the trace disappears, did it have past existence? Think about the x, then forget it. If the x is gone without remainder, what happens in the interval?

The archaeology of thought excavates what the present has rejected

Not knowing if a thing is real is not a reason to deny what it is

What is the difference between a perception and a vivid recollection? We say, the perception has an object but all we have to go on is the perception.

Hallucination may seem real but not object-like in its realness

The feeling of realness does not depend on the "reality" of the object

Unlike the limitless expanse of wakefulness, the curved space of dream provides a model for the universe. In the same sense, the palpable space of dream does not suggest an empty container.

Thought occurs without a self in some unconscious states, but a self cannot occur without a conscious thought.

There is awareness of objects and activities in animals and young children but no intentional consciousness without a self

Objects parse subjective space across a bridge of consciousness. In opposition to events outside, the self recurs to see them

We think that thinking instigates the actions that we think about, but a thought is a finality.

Thought and memory

The phase of thought does not initiate action but is a bottleneck on acts.

In the path from self to speech, thought is incomplete perception, while action is completed thought. We see this more clearly in the verbalization of inner speech.

Is a thought an incomplete object or an action forestalled?

> Are traces of childhood pain
> Early structures in the brain?

When recollection does not reach a conscious phase, persuaded by what we can't remember, we act on memories we have forgotten.

Is memory doubled to recognize insufficiency? I mean, how do we know a memory is inaccurate if we do not have an unconscious template to compare with?

Actually, there is no comparison, just a feeling of incompleteness

A false memory is an errant thought. Thought creeps in where memory falters. It arises as a departure from recollection.

Perceptions are memories on the chopping block of sensibility

Though a feeling can revive a memory, events are usually recalled with greater clarity than feelings

I am often confused when something comes to mind, not knowing if it was an experience, a thought, a dream, half-imaged or half-real

Don't think so hard, thought comes unbidden.

Concentration does not select content; it prevents distraction

Do not seek a certain thought. Be patient and it will find you

In line with necessity, the hand of memory makes voluntary gestures

Immediacy is a truce of actuality with the unreal

The consummation of memory is the re-creation of the now

Thoughts slip the net of actuality for life in the unknown world

The noose of certainty tinged with surprise, slithers through cracks to the surface

I can see why others think my theory implausible, but do they ever question theirs?

The *cogito* is: I exist because the recurrence of memory thinks me up

For the substance thinker, change is the problem. For the process thinker, stability. The resolution is becoming-into-being.

If time was reversed, being would be becoming and the world would be invisible.

Habitual thinking prevents imaginative growth. Even if the past is not consciously recalled, it keeps revisiting.

Having given up on the living, I write for the dead and the unborn.

Is one difference of memory and thought who I was and who I am?

A retardation of growth is the key to intellectual advance

In the category of thinking, creative thought is an active blocking of the old or irrelevant and a readiness for surprise.

Thought achieves closure in propositions but is more alive when wordless.

Thoughts tap the potential of images in a shift from spatial wholes to temporal parts.

The parts—words, notes, symbols—are dead artifacts when the antecedent thoughts are not evoked.

I can picture the girls I loved long ago but not the young man who loved them.

The simple and the complex

Accepting the ambiguity in every thought is a deeper form of understanding.

SIMPLICITY IS AVOIDING ENTANGLEMENT in unnecessary complexity. Often it rests in dismissing irrelevance to isolate the essential. It can be equated with parsimony, though this can mean a collapse of richness to one variable. For the gullible, complexity is a sufficient explanation of uncertainty. Just to postulate complexity is to admit confusion for what the complexity stands for, and to give up striving for simplicity. We can choose to ignore one perspective in favor of another or accept that both are insoluble.

∾

The mother of precision casts a shadow of doubt on every fact.

Intelligence may not rule wisely but stupidity is worse. The most important attribute is simplicity of character

The avocation of philosophers is to elaborate complexity in simple ideas

There is simplicity at the beginning and the end, and a tangle of complexity in-between

A simple truth can only be appreciated by explaining what it conceals. Even a platitude requires a volume of explication.

We hesitate to make a choice, even if choices are given. That is, we do not choose our choices. They arise when specification is postponed. In action, delay allows contemplation of an outcome, often until it is too late to act. This is not thinking too slowly. When deliberation replaces spontaneity, the inner life predominates.

My thought is glacial interspersed with occasional wit. I suffer from want of cleverness, an *esprit d'escalier* after the conversation has moved on. Perhaps I write to record those moments when it was too late to speak.

The appeal of paradox is paradoxical. The analytic trend aims at resolution.

Precision is close approximation

We pursue specificity but wisdom is satisfied with the ambiguity that gave rise to specificity in the first place.

How do we explain why the certainty in a true fact is provisional, while the conviction for error is unshakeable?

What is Mañjuśrī getting at? To know this is to begin to understand

> A profound truth, Niels Bohr said,
> May conceal a greater truth instead
> When contradictions both are true
> Synthesis unites the two

Still, he must have grown dyspeptic with his taste for dialectic
Synthesis is a novel outlook in the shadow of polarities.
The progression from synthesis to analysis has antithesis falling aside
Action is the negation of inaction but inaction is also action.
The contrast that isolates an object from what it is not is the foundation of dialectic.
The problem is to find an antithesis other than negation.
A natural synthesis is not the blending of oppositions but the finding of a common ground.
Precision is a stern judge of the ambiguity that fosters new ideas.

Depth

The deepest thought can usually find the words.
The deepest feeling is ineffable.

THE CONCEPT OF DEPTH originates as a spatial concept in the experience of levels in the external world; a deep well, cave, a river, or the sky. Depth also has a temporal dimension. It relates to the immediate and the distant, as in the depth of the past. Depth also refers to the mystical unseen and the surface immediacy, to the evident or visible and the imperceptible, as in a subterranean root and a palpable leaf.

We can also speak of a person's depth as well, the psychological depth of the unconscious: depth of thought, feeling, insight. This is in opposition to superficial or surface thought or behavior. Is this a metaphor for depth in the external world or does it capture an important relation? It seems to me that psychological depth entails hierarchy and simultaneity of levels such that phenomena can be attributed to earlier or later at the same moment, or in the same mental state.

An animal that behaves consistent with its evolutionary stage does not display depth in behavior, even though there is a micro-temporal transition from instinct to action. Similarly, we do not speak of the unconscious of animals

However, early expressions of phylogenetic stages in human anatomy or cognition are attributed to deep structure in thought or brain. In this idea of depth earlier stages are inferred to give rise to later ones. When depth refers to the process of thought, the implication is that conscious thought and behavior derive from antecedents that are more or less concurrent with their outcomes.

The term "profound" implies depth as well, though it relates to intricacy. The assumption is that a deep or profound thinker is operating at

Reflections on Mind and the Image of Reality

more preliminary phases of greater complexity; phases that are intuitive, subjective, and less determined by immediate or extrinsic events.

Depth and breadth are commonly associated, though not necessarily related. A deep argument in mathematics, as with the Fermat theorem, can be restricted to a relatively narrow set of problems. However in psychology, and in other fields—linguistics, physics, economics—the greater the depth, the more holistic the ground of the argument and the greater generality in application of the seminal idea.

For example in transformational grammar, depth refers to the kernel of an utterance or to grammatical competence, while surface refers to performance or production in speech. In all or most instances, intermediate levels or grades of realization are acknowledged. In systems theory, depth can also refer to the level to which phenomena are reduced. The account of a mental event is considered deeper if reduced to brain, genome or physics. In microgenetic theory, depth refers to potential, to the preliminary, the unconscious, the instinctual or drive-related; surface to actuality, to conscious imagery, action and objects.

∾

The impression of depth often owes to silence, not speech

Fluency can appear rehearsed or glib, while slowness of speech and hesitation, justly or not, may imply greater depth of thought. One has the sense that speech is word-close or thought-close.

Ambiguity implies depth more than precision. The relation is uncertainty to finality.

The risk in speaking is not only that it uncovers what is left unspoken. The commitment to one line of discourse aborts the potential for others.

Creative exploration of the submerged is obviated in discharge to speech.

Some thinkers achieve depth or profundity by allusion. The attempt to uncover depth without articulating it avoids closure in statements.

Ordinarily, speech reveals limits in thinking, since we know more than we can say

The more we try to explain an idea, the further we drift from its power. This is often the distinction of intuition and proof, or concept and data.

One sign of depth is compression, as in poetry or mathematics. This is why Wittgenstein seems deeper than Russell.

Emotions that run deep do not overflow but are felt in what is left unexpressed

Deep time condensed in brain development is retraced in every momentary state.

The animal past of instinctual drive is deep but not profound. Here, deep means earlier, stronger, more global, not intricate or original.

We might say a habit is deeply ingrained. This implies that it arises early in life and cognition.

Originality is deep if it touches on more than the thinker intended.

Depth is the generality in a profound truth.

To find the depth in an original formulation one has to abandon words

Water is murky in the deepest well and clearest at the surface. Careful in descent you don't fall in.

The mystical is a sign that thought has run out of certainty

Depth and surface are not on the same level but occur at the same time.

Since all phases are entrained in every act of cognition, depth and surface point to the dominant locus of thought.

The deepest river has turbulence at the surface; Richard Feynman on the bongo drums.

Jung was deeper than Freud, but Freud had wider scope. The difference between them is like Beethoven and Mozart.

☙

If you look too closely at something, it may become repellant. A butterfly is not beautiful under a magnifying glass. Or I should say the beauty that appeals to everyone is, to a scientist, the beauty of functional organization. The one is beauty-external in the immediacy of the visual; the other is beauty-internal in order and harmony. The surface impression is near-universal; deeper appreciation requires particular knowledge. But is the deeper response still that of beauty? Does the beauty of a sunset survive if one sees only astronomical data? Beauty can be destroyed—or enhanced—by knowledge. It requires a penumbra of awe or wonder at what is known, and a sense of mystery in what is not.

☙

To concentrate on the mystical without the benefit of fact betrays a superficial understanding.

Though astronauts have walked its pitted landscape, lovers still swoon in the moonlight.

Like a butterfly, the moon is beautiful from a distance when unperturbed by science.

If only the initiated can appreciate the beauty in science, does this also apply to religion and the mystical?

What has universal appeal is certainly not deep, but the deepest ideas are universal.

Asked why such and such is the case, one can only cite posterior data. The final why is unanswerable.

The profound thinker does not ask why things are the way they are, but still goes on explaining. Yet explanation does not give the ultimate why.

> Hard to reply
> Without telling a lie
> Never a doubt
> Much is left out
>
> Competitors said it
> But he took credit
> No need to regret it
> Since others forget it.
>
> What we want may not be who we are.
> What we need may not be what we want
>
> Cynicism may be justified but trust is more likely to give happiness
> The residue of what is said includes its antithesis
> Love is not ineffable but the language has not yet been invented
> Life spews ancient wisdom snatched from predatory jaws
> The wise man predicts the future after it arrives

Absence

Better to say, I am the space that otherwise would be unoccupied

IS THERE EVER NOTHING, or is nothing a something one cannot name? An image, say of a unicorn, is something. My not being somewhere is still something, though the where-I-am-not could be thought of as nothing. Yet, still that is a portion of space. Nothing is not non-existence. Fairies and elves are something but do not exist. My death will convert me to a not-nothing as the body decays to something else, though my mind will be nothing unless, implausibly, it continues as soul. Who can think on nothingness? In life, when I am absent, I am present somewhere else. How is this absence different if I am dead or if others do not know if I am dead or alive?

∽

There are no degrees of nothing; emptiness is not a quantity,

The space you occupy is insubstantial, a vanishing point

Mark Strand wrote, "*In a field I am the absence of field*". What fills that absence when Strand is elsewhere?

This is not quite right. You create the space, including that which your body occupies.

A spatial image of your body is the space your body is in

Empty space is also an object. I move my arm and slice through an invisible soup. We learn this from the palpable space of dream

The mystics do not believe a not-nothing comes from nothing, only that it precedes a something.

God is the only something from which a not-nothing can arise

Two-dimensional space is a timeless flatland; the third dimension gives transition

If the two-dimensional face of an object is approaching, is there a lapse of time in the depth of its approach?

If depth in space is analogous to duration in time, time as a fourth dimension is forecast in three-dimensional space.

We think of existence in spatial terms though it is occurrence and recurrence in time. If time is recurrent, non-existence is non-recurrence, though a particle with an extremely brief duration exists. Still, the person I was a moment ago and the world in which I appeared no longer exist, having been replaced by the next moment.

Do events have to occur in some present to exist?

Is the past non-existent, or is it an eternal (Platonic) object? Perhaps the entire history of the universe is one moment in the present of god's mind.

Does the fact that objects are replaced, or change to something else, mean they no longer exist, or does everything have some place in the simultaneity of a timeless space?

If space has three or more dimensions, does time have more than one?

If the physical space between entities is empty, what of the mental space between illusory objects? Is mental space a representation or a kind of thing? If so, to what does it correspond in physical space?

Focal brain damage separately affects objects in space and experience in time. What should this tell us about the spatialization of time in physics?

Variables

*Every moment entails a covert decision.
The greater part of a life consists of constant decisions
made without thinking.*

THE MIND AND THE world contain so many variables that impact behavior it is surprising only one option is selected. To go to a film is influenced by the quality, reviews, length, actors, hour, duration, weather, companionship, schedule for tomorrow, and so on, all of which reduce to yes or no. How is this explained? Does each of these variables undergo a covert decision that contributes to, and is absorbed in, the overall feeling that leads to yes or no? Often, on such occasions, we suddenly decide one way or another without a conscious inventory of pluses and minuses, rather like a person with a list of qualities they want in a partner, perhaps using it to justify solitariness or rejecting potential suitors, then discarding it when the right person comes along.

There is a tendency to extract one variable from a set—generally a dichotomy—and explain the set in terms of the variable. A typical strategy is to select one feature of brain activity—synthesis, abstraction, integration, re-entry—and explain all activity on this basis. With respect to optimism and pessimism, the variable is positive and negative. This variable has been used to explain a great number of phenomena, from excitation and inhibition in the brain, on/off, yes/no, the digitalization of thought, approach/avoidance, aggression/defense, fight/flight, love/hate, affirmation/denial, and so on. This simplifies complexity and boils down to the two routes of action available in most situations, but it relegates the richness of experience to the go/no go of immediate action.

One way to view this thought-sequence is as a set of binary choices that bias the final decision. Each possible reason to go or not to go is evaluated and, on balance or as the greater sum, the final decision is made. This supposes a sequence of positive/negative choice that determines the final decision. However, a person who feels ill on a cold and rainy night, asked to see a film s/he knows will be terrible, is excited to go just to be with the other person. Here, one variable—the companion—trumps all others. Where is the logic in that?

Indeed, the most compelling motivation might be boredom and the lack of anything else to do; that is, something other than nothing. One question is whether this analysis occurs more or less instantaneously prior to a decision, or the decision is prior to the analysis providing a retroactive justification for whatever action is taken. The larger question concerns the act of decision itself, and what role it plays in action. If the final conscious act results from a veto (Libet) of competing possibilities, the agent does not so much choose but rather, the process of choice cancels alternatives, such that the decision is less for what to do than for what not to do. The resultant is not the selection of an option but a pruning of virtual acts that for one reason or another do not prevail. The elimination of alternatives feels like a commitment to the option that remains, while a legitimate choice might be accompanied by a residue of doubt.

On this interpretation, the different factors that go into a decision about a film are subsumed in a category of experiential memory, similar to those grouped about going to work, a party or a picnic. These categories are initially limited but enlarge over multiple occasions. Features of the category—actors in the film, responsibilities at work, a dress, ants—play a greater or lesser role, and each has an affective charge. When the occasion arises, the experiential category is evoked, items—initially virtual and subliminal—are elicited and decision is made depending on the emotional valence of any one of them.

∾

"I used to be indecisive but now I'm not so sure". Probably, decisiveness increases with age as likes and dislikes solidify.

We think indecision is weakness when it may be greater knowledge, excessive caution or competing intensities.

I am decisive for that which I care about and indifferent to the rest. What is crucial is the proportion.

If indifference is the greatest sin (Oscar Wilde), what of those who are exercised by everything?

If I give up striving, I give up caring.

Variables

A sleeping dog is immediately excited by its master, by food, a walk, another dog. There is no decision, only the pleasure of the activity. Does this primitive layer gird human decision-making?

Some go along with everything like leaves in the wind. What is lacking in this passive attitude? We might say lack of confidence but how is this explained?

The passive and the active are distinct at an early age. Some think the strength of the infant grasp reflex is an indicator.

With little knowledge, decision, like opinion, comes easily. This is because the affective charge within a category is concentrated on a few items.

At times I decide to write when I have nothing to write about, and then the writing comes. Making a decision activates the ground of what the decision is about. The need overcomes a seeming absence of incipient thought

If you can't decide, act; then adjust to what comes.

To change your mind is for something—experience, feeling—to alter the predictability of unconscious choice.

I didn't want to go but am glad I did. This is common enough, but why?

The little decisions she made accumulated; the big ones left to me rarely came. Eventually, I realized I was living her life.

He dropped so many names I needed a broom to clean up.

Sit down, stand up, glass of water, which glass, walk here, walk there; unconscious choices, not carrots leading the mule.

Imagine having to decide every momentary act, as if the heart should decide to beat every second. When choice becomes conscious, be grateful that habit kicks in.

Traveling widely, one becomes un-situated, so the self, independent of locus, is the sole center of identity.

Conscious indecision is incomplete specification. It is less the competing ideas than their opposing affective charge that delays resolution and arouses introspection. Habit eases the transition to definiteness.

The unconscious is not a storehouse from which items are selected. The derivation to consciousness is facilitated by concentration, which impedes distraction, and by uncertainty, which retards transition.

Repression and denial

*The method is simple. Sniff out the infantile
wish buried like a dog's bone.*

TO THE AVERAGE PERSON, repression implies that content is actively restrained from coming into consciousness, like sweeping an unpleasant thought or urge under the rug. However, because something doesn't come up that does not mean it is necessarily prevented from doing so. We do not speak of difficulty finding a word, recalling a name, or in "split-brain" cases, content that cannot be verbalized as repressed. Repression presumes a mechanism that represses.

The idea of repression is bogus but it is the linchpin of psychiatric theory and practice. Freud proposed the withdrawal of drive energy from the memory trace, not as an active suppression but a passive release, a detachment. How unconscious energy locates the trace in the first place is as mysterious as how it detaches itself from it. More likely, category and feeling are part of the same developing construct, with inability to achieve consciousness a result of state-specificity or failure of individuation. Normally, the progression to definiteness in the subjective portion of mind continues outward to sensibility in its objective portion, with most people unaware that the outer is a sensory modification of the inner.

The path of survival will never lead to an understanding of the mind. Evolution has millions of years to conceal what we have only a few to uncover, as ancestral illusions that mirror the world so closely we do not recognize them unless they appear out of context. Illusions adapt to reality to generate a world so accurate we presume it is real and ignore its phenomenal quality. We assign objects to the world and allocate thought and feeling to the mind, a coping strategy instilled over millions of years to create an implicit model of reality.

Repression and denial

Insanity is the price for knowledge of the real, perhaps a warning to stick to concrete fact, leaving speculation at the doorstep and avoiding a too-hasty conviction. The schizophrenic feels the truth of philosophical idealism that a world of hallucinatory images is carved by sensation to an adaptive model. The hallucinations and delusions of the psychotic are not mere distortions; they expose mind-internal, and the incompleteness of the continuum to external objects when sensory constraints are ineffective or overwhelmed. The illness peels away the crust of mind to uncover the subjective origin of the world. In schizophrenia, terror results from loss of agency, estrangement, the realness of imagery and the gap to reality; though it is unlikely a veridical world can be recollected We do not need little homunculi to explain the workings of the (unconscious) mind if we can understand that symptoms are accentuations of what is normally submerged. Thus, paranoia gives rise to the self of dream, a self which is passive to image-content. This dream-self surfaces *in lieu* of the waking self—the active self— as a victim to its own thoughts and objects.

If denial is conscious, one must be aware of it, and then it is not actually "denied". If, as argued, it is unconscious, how are the events to be denied selected? My view is that painful memories may remain unconscious not because they are denied but because there is a strong affective tonality that cannot partition to the affect-ideas of conscious thought.

༄

Although my theory is closer to Jung than Freud, it is the lesser known Paul Schilder who was the most brilliant.

Freud saw behaviors as revealing unconscious structure. Errors with brain damage are the same, though commonly viewed as a loss of mechanism.

Psychoanalysis is exorcism lauded as science. It fills the mind with demons, then profits by getting rid of them

The distinction of latent and manifest in dream is critical, as Freud foresaw. The manifest is the pre-object, the being; the latent is the process, the becoming.

Psychoanalysis holds that sleep is protected by dream. If so, why are my awakenings invariably during a dream?

A mental complex is justification for childhood abuse as fantasy

A wet foot in the unconscious prods the dry bones of memory (Oedipus)

Sexual pleasure is compensation for life's distress paid for by the next generation

Reflections on Mind and the Image of Reality

Knowing the nature of mind does not guarantee contentment. In fact, once awareness sets in, insight can ruin your life

The schizophrenic feels the truth that reason thinks it knows

The realness of an image shatters a thin veneer of sanity

The doors of perception, closed in dream, opened by the senses, porous to imagery, traversed by objects

Seeing a chair melt away in the soup of mental space shakes the common belief that what we see is real

A frantic colleague taking drugs, now mumbling in the nuthouse, sent his "astral body" on a voyage to the cosmos; unfortunately, not a round-trip.

> I spent a year reading Ezra Pound, snake in the grass
> At St. Elizabeth's, schizophrenic wisdom
> In murky waters, adored by writers,
> A stinking mess, threw his feces on the wall

Vertigo affects the image to uncover a mind-dependent world

Looking at the object will not help. Close your eyes and its nature will be clear

Enlightenment for those who live in darkness is still a kind of twilight

The world is what you think, not what you think it is

In sunlight we live in shadows. Step aside to see what is obscured

When the implicit seems real, the mind is already in danger

Know that to feel the real is a warning sign of illness

The realness of dream is closer to waking than the reality of objects that only seem real

Knowledge of the world requires a conspiracy of senses

The opposite of real is knowable, The opposite of reality is absence

If reality is inferred from illusion, how is the real sustained? If a world is created in the mind, on what does reality depend?

> The meanings we seek are phantoms etched in human brain,
> A sign the trickster is at work.

Consciousness is the arc of the intentional.

> An enthusiast of Hume
> Might be forgiven to assume
> That no matter how insistent
> The self is non-existent

Repression and denial

Okay, the self is an illusion. But why stop there?

An object is a film between the unconscious and reality

An object fits a niche, the levo and the dextro, doubly hard to know, like a footprint in the sand, a negative image of the real.

The beloved, a mirror between the mind of a lover and nature: a reflection on either side.

If we saw everything as in a mirror, we would adapt to reversal and life would go on. But this is what happens normally.

An upside down world with inverting lenses rights itself after some days. Even an illusory adaptation is a real property.

> For Anatman theory to be sustained
> It has to be explained
> How the illusion is maintained

The Buddhists give up striving, but even a rock aims at replication
If everything is illusion, it is hopeless to penetrate the veil,
Among the illusions, die only for love
The limit of knowledge is our model of reality
As the cocoon of the material opens, the infant enters a dream
The shades of those departed are still shadows when alive
Philosophy and neuroscience scavenge the clinic for curiosities to reinforce a claim, but often clinicians do the same.

Freud had the virtue of presenting opposing arguments, but only those that were not decisive.

All the world's a stage

*A successful life depends on how well,
and how convincing, each role is played.*

THE GREATER THE ART of the actor, the less it seems like acting. We all play many roles in life, over time or in a day—son, husband, father, lover, teacher—each exhibiting a nuance of personality and, in most instances, except in gradations of the Jekyll-Hyde continuum, a steadiness of character. One role may require forcefulness and competition, another tenderness and affection, still another, treachery and deceit. Some roles are a disguise, others unavoidable, most natural. The degree of pretense depends on how fully the behavior taps the personality. The great actor draws on reserves of experience that expand the potential of expression. A successful life depends on how well, and how convincing, each role is played. The person is often unaware of role-playing when the behavior is a facet of personality. When I was a practicing doctor, the role involved a conscious assumption of a comportment that would meet the expectations of patients and family, at times insincere but essential to my profession.

A lecture is also a performance that is judged by an audience no less than an actor in a drama. If the performance is adept, an authenticity comes through that carries to the audience a conviction in the ideas that are exchanged. Is the argument true, is the conclusion persuasive, can we trust its veracity? In all fields, there are charlatans that sell themselves and their message to a public gullible or uninformed. Like a performance on stage, a lecture is, to a great extent, scripted and repeated on many occasions to a different audience, whether a teacher in a classroom or a politician on the stump. The fact that each of the many roles a person plays can alternate over the course of hours points to an inclusiveness and plasticity of the personality, or in some, a susceptibility to influence. This makes one wonder as to the nature, composition and repeatability of the self.

Consider cases of "multiple personality", in which many, even dozens, of distinct alters (selves) have been identified; though some experts are dubious and assert that the selves trace to a unified self-concept. One psychiatrist (Herb Spiegel) who studied the famous case of Sibil, believed the common factor was suggestibility, linking it to the ease with which a person could be hypnotized. He once put it to me that when he rode his horse he felt like John Wayne. It was a short step to feeling like "big John" and identifying with the actor. Fusion tends to occur when the insurance runs out. The multiple is impressionable to the point of self-hypnosis. This implies that the empirical self is more amenable to, or alterable by, external conditions, while the core self, prior to conscious awareness, remains relatively unchanged.

In my view, the core self is a subliminal category of instinctual drive and implicit belief; a relatively stable (recurrent) construct derived to a conscious empirical self that adapts to situational immediacy. The multiplicity of adaptive possibilities—an ordinary person coping with circumstance, a psychopath or personality disorder—are manifestations of the explicit or conscious self as a category of implementations of the subliminal core. In contrast, the consciousness of role in most ordinary people implies sensitivity to the authenticity of the core, which is lacking in the multiple. A role is an adaptive strategy that is usually determined by external conditions, as when a mature adult feels like a child on visiting his parents, or a shift in personality and attendant features when acting as a doctor, lawyer, professor etc.

The plasticity of the empirical self owes to the potential in the core. Given its proximity to instinctual drive, this potential is similar in most people, though expressed with a greater or lesser capacity to adapt to different situations. As the core arises in drive, the aggressive and defensive tendencies of hunger—greed, ambition, abstinence, love, desire, perversion—bias the conscious self according to instinctual and adaptive need. For example, sexual behavior is framed by an active, acquisitive attitude or a passive, dependent one, which develops out of the vectors of fight and flight. At a simple level, one manifestation of the self is driven by an outgoing tendency, another is submissive or tolerant, e.g. confidence or shyness, each an implementation of the core through which all behaviors are filtered. The individuation of these tendencies in relation to experience and innate disposition leads to a wide diversity of personality type.

In sum, the unconscious self is a category that partitions to a conscious self that is biased by the core and closer to behavior in the world. The influence of the unconscious self is mitigated in consciousness, which progressively narrows and weakens in the transition to adaptive behavior. However, the self as a category embraces many possible derivations (e.g. vindictive, forgiving, generous, acquisitive, and so on, all attributes of personality that accommodate inner need to outer circumstance). The psychic "distance" between the categories of the conscious and unconscious self may account for the awareness of authenticity in action.

~

Though my personality is a complex of possibilities and roles, I never wonder who I am.

The self is elusive because it cannot be the object of a consciousness that it anchors and instigates. The self is the proximal category in an arc of consciousness that passes through introspection to the world.

We know our self by our thoughts and acts, not by observation.

If one probes deep into mind, like Hume or James, the self cannot be uncovered. This is because the self is doing the probing.

Why would a self that is illusory, think it is an illusion?

In conversation with another, there is always the question of which self I am speaking to.

If I were to have multiple encapsulated selves, I would not ask if they are unified. Each self is all there is in the duration of its occurrence.

If a series of partitions leads to a different self, what could be the common thread to an authentic one? Presumably it is the diachronic process of origination.

The category of a self is a composite of potential individuations, some more prominent than others, but each role contributes to the sense of who a person is.

The loss of some constituent of the self—spouse, health, career—is like an excision of that mode of self-realization. The contraction of the category limits the range of its derivations.

Over time, the self can be reconstituted if one accepts or replaces a lost realization.

There is a period of mourning for the loss, which can be life-altering. Cases of trauma to the cervical spine with quadriplegia often go through a psychotic stage in the restitution of the self-concept.

Of course in dying there is loss of all possibilities of self-realization without replacement, though it might be easier if one constituent of myself was the imaginary self (soul) of an afterlife.

When someone says, I was not myself the implication is an act that is out of character, not the expression of a different personality.

Character is the constancy extracted from personality, which is variability in the expression of character.

PART II

The Emotional Animal

How do we separate personal and impersonal experience?

Otherness

It is too easy to dehumanize others, whom we see as objects.
What is remarkable is to humanize them,
inferring a mind like our own.

WE ALL HAVE A sense of otherness, explicit or subdued, or conceived abstractly as alienation, solitariness, the tragedy of life, a confrontation with others or ideas. More concretely, it is a font of jealousy, aggravation and resentment, of family, neighbors, colleagues, religions, ethnic groups, differences of community, class, tribes, or national identity. Polarization is a natural tendency of mind oblivious to transition and unhinged from mitigating factors. The transition to the outer deposits a world as the imposition of sensibility on emerging mental contents. The abruptness results in separation and apartness. The individual gazes on and acts in a world that appears outside mind. An exaggeration of the difference of inner and outer, and an enclosure of the self in a space helmet confines the individual to a private landscape of memory and feeling that separates itself from a world that is independent and unforgiving. The individual can be an instigator or target, an object or a mind, one that initiates or reacts. Self and thought are the principal loci of internal interest, while the world and its contents are an external source of danger, opportunity and confrontation.

Not only is beauty in the eye of the beholder but so is everything else. The feelings, character and beliefs we infer in others are conditioned by our own. An incongruity of subjective image and material object accounts for disappointment and betrayal. The demonization of others depends on treating the other as a category of like types, or isolating the individual as an ideal (of evil, goodness). The same process occurs in love, except that, in the former, a need that is reinforced by others overcomes doubt and hesitation. We see this when utopian ideals replace reason and personal experience. The critical link is value. In love, it settles in an idea (ideal) embodied in a particular (the beloved). In political life, it settles in an idea, or ideal (e.g. social justice), that represents a group or a grievance.

One implication of this line of thought is that any social model that posits external conflict as a natural or non-manufactured outcome of the subject/object relation, fails to address the social nature of human experience or to allocate responsibility for its disruption to instigators of otherness by agitation and self-interest. An individual is a momentary actualization of core beliefs and values, instilled or inherited, who may be shy or outspoken, timid or aggressive, solitary or social, but while the subject-to-object transition and the imposition of sensibility lead to a separation of self and other (world), and can enable a militant apartness—survival requires a struggle with the external—there is nothing in the internal sequence of the actualization process that disposes to conflict. Alienation tends to be a condition of unhinged writers and armchair theorists. Humans, like Bonobos, are for the most part social animals.

The point is, the formative process from core to surface in mind is an individuation of categorical wholes, i.e. potential to actual, while external events are interpreted as causally related. When external objects are internalized, mind is conceived as a camp of warring ideas (logical solids), interpreted along the lines of external objects, that is, in conflict. A more relevant question is: why individual mental states are so susceptible to influence? Say, to strong political opinion, such that the person can be persuaded to assimilate the ideology and implement the will of others, malevolent or benign, relinquishing all prudence and perspective. In this respect, the follower is equally an object as those he despises.

Capitalism is depicted as brutal Darwinism, but it is actually symbiotic with psychic process through the specification of acts and ideas and the adaptation of needs to circumstance (act, object). This is not internal contestation but a pruning of maladaptive possibilities. An implicit falling-away of the unrealized does not entail competitors. Attitudes have differing occasions of satisfaction, with creative solutions to novel circumstances. Inequality of achievement is not injustice, no more than good or bad luck. Darwinian speciation occurs in final objects, i.e. populations, not actualities forming in human mind. An alternative to Capitalism, Socialism, is motivated not by justice but envy, bucking the trend of mentality, perhaps a reason for its relative failure. In sum, conflict occurs in the world among final objects, not in the mind, except when ideas objectify as logical solids.

Otherness

Mental process is the recurrent individuation of particulars. Conflict in mind is ordinarily indecision, not opposition.

∽

Recurrence is not a facsimile. Ingredient novelty is the hope for constant renewal.

> If one looks coldly at the facts
> Can someone say they saw
> The love so rare in human acts
> In the world of tooth and claw?

A person as an object and a mind as a process are both targets of opportunity.

Others are infantilized by self-serving givers

Treating a person as a victim is a theft of self-empowerment

Action signals character, but a good man can be betrayed by a lack of courage.

The secret Nazi is surely deplorable but what of an exemplary character afraid to act?

Sartre said we are the sum of our acts. Is there no difference between the inaction of a bigot and an altruist?

I am a leader with no followers. Is it because I am unable to simplify?

Wordsworth's "against all enemies prepared, all except neglect" comes to mind.

The good teacher does not propagandize; he protects students against the hegemony of his ideas

Whoever is insufficiently aggressive to enjoy power or overly diffident to seek it will languish in bitter obscurity.

The leader intoxicates followers by empowering their inadequacies.

We are all indoctrinated, but the courageous follow their own ideas

A mob first assimilates the values of members, then implements them.

The conscious person arises in a communal unconscious. The subordination of the will to a mob occurs when the self sinks into the category from which it arose.

Make an object of a person to dehumanize him before an attack

To attack others for a dubious cause, though graver, is no less a weakness than to do nothing for a righteous one. One actor is an instrument of the will of the mob; the other lacks a will of his own.

Ridicule is a cheap but effective weapon in the armament of scoundrels

Becoming the other in love can be replaced by identification with a community of others. In both, the self is relinquished.

In love, the creation of an ideal is a concentration of value in a focality of interest; in political life, value concentrates in an idea by the suppression of competing perspectives.

Instead of the deep union of self and other in love, why is the surface contact of discourse so often oppositional?

Fidelity to an idea or movement is stronger than to a lover. An idea is reinforced by others, love by reciprocity in spite of others

It is rare that opposing ideas inhabit the mind of one individual

A well-founded opinion takes opposing views into consideration.

A belief is not a fixed idea but a tendency. The fixation comes when the potential in the belief is overcome by an habitual attitude

In the tendency to polarities, the unity of belief that partitions to duality is foreclosed in opinion

Choices not in the same category do not represent opposing beliefs. The difficulty is not with ideas but the belief system in which they are embedded

The more articulated the idea, the more ingrained, the less tolerant of refutation.

Depth of belief is not bound to conviction. Strong opinions appear superficial but resist argumentation

Does an opinion express a belief, a value or habitual thinking?

It may be easier to refute certain beliefs than opinions

The generality of a belief gives the locality of opinion, like an approaching murmur that becomes a shrill noise.

Once belief is committed to a statement, opinion hardens and possibilities are lost

Those who would mitigate action or avoid commitment turn to history as an excuse

I do not much care what you think, only why you think it

I am not strongly opinionated. Is this a sign of weak character or an open mind?

We are entitled to the truth, not to our opinions. But to what ground must we appeal?

The wisdom of aging is acceptance

Would the world be better if we recognized the triviality of most pursuits, the banality of most decisions and the futility of most causes?

Otherness

 The only cure for the boredom of life is a passion, no matter what it is for

∾

 In those with unhealthy attitudes, to conspire against stereotypes or confer on others idealizations of power is a costly artifact of the colonization of human psyche. A curiosity of mental process is the solidification of extremes. The diversity of subjective aim reflects a differing emphasis on inner and outer, subject or object, values, ideals and categorical thinking. Behaviors are influenced by the deception of boundaries, (self/world, object/event), by the different quality of the subjective and objective, and by insensitivity to continua, which are buried in the stability of things, properties, persons, attributes, points of view. Love is a bridge to the other and a destroyer of otherness, but when self-assertion predominates, the other dissolves in otherness, and love is a mere emollient. This teaches us that the peaks are never so steep, the valleys never so low, even if the continuum is invisible. The possibility of love reminds us that, so far as possible, we should treat the other as a *Thou* (Buber).

∾

 A subtle choreography is at work in the grove of palms swaying in the breeze

 In mind, conflict is indecision; in the world, competition

 Individuality is the freedom to act; generality is the wisdom to know what to do

 Instances replace categories, particulars obscure universals

 Synthesis to analysis is the natural trend. The reverse is inauthentic

 Not surprisingly, people gesture while talking on the phone. The imaginary other is still in the room

 We are like fish out of water gasping for air oblivious to the invisible beyond

 Life happens between the possible and the irrevocable

 It took twenty years to write Ulysses, Joyce said, and should take twenty to read it

> Students said they understood
> I wondered how they could
> In one quick year inculcate
> What took some thirty to create

Reflections on Mind and the Image of Reality

Cashing out a single life, the genome was devised to multiply diversity
The tree of life is bottomless, the leaves infinite, the root one
A good reason to seek the inner eye is to replenish the perishing of outward gaze

>Categories of self and now
>Durations in the ceaseless flow
>A bubble for the self to know
>What lies ahead, what lies below

On love

Is there a union of the heart that is not a meeting of the minds?
Is love a soliloquy or a conversation?

ONE PLUS ONE IS forever two, but in love, one is not a number; it is oneness, unity or wholeness. Love creates and absorbs the other as a novel whole. The magic of love is one becoming two without an addition. In this respect, there is a difference in the wholeness of lovers and the shared ideal of friendship, one as two, two as one.

The immediacy of loving contrasts with the detachment of writing. The latter engages the memory of love to evoke the feeling and not the presence of the beloved. Yet, even in the presence of the beloved, the source of inner feeling is still in the imagination, and in genuine love it is in the ideal. However, I can feel love in writing about it since in the imagination there is little separation between the self and object, even if the intensity of feeling competes with the effort in finding the words of love to evoke the feeling. Writing is an embodiment of feeling in words, as loving is in intimacy and sexuality. It is also a way of reviving the other, though writing filters the insubstantial into words.

When love begins as an encounter, rarely do we ask: will the other remain one among many or become an ideal and repository? The bland togetherness of surface contacts leads to a kind of attachment, but superficial "connections" do not engage the fabric of the ideal.

How is feeling exchanged? You don't catch it like a cold. Many assume that a couple comes together in an agreeable manner with common interests, that feeling grows over time and at some point the couple declares they are in love. Is this accurate? What part is played by imagery, desire, need? What, if any, are the boundaries of attachment? How does absence aggravate wish? Most couples after passion subsides lapse into numb habit, filling boredom with more boredom as Schopenhauer wrote. Affection, adoration, adulation, passion, compatibility, compassion, not to mention devotion or obsession, reveal the relation of inner to outer, or the extent to which objects and the imagination are in play.

Imagination and idealization blur imperfections and heighten qualities of attraction that are the kernel of romantic love. Though sexuality achieves the evanescent oneness that was hoped for in the partition of the self, the essence of love is prolonged and intensified in the imagination rather than in the company of the beloved. To think of, to imagine or to recall the beloved evokes feelings of love similar in intensity to being in the presence of the beloved.

In the presence of the other, our feelings lose power to the toxic forces of inspection, analysis and rational judgment. Loving accommodates to adaptation, resolving the real with the ideal. There is a sanctity in romantic imagery that cannot always be sustained in the company of the beloved, where there can be tumult, arguments or fits of jealousy. In imagery, love is more intense—if less real—but the unreal of the imaginary is what love and writing are about.

All of this is to say that love differs when I am alone, thinking or writing, from when I am with my beloved. Alone I am my whole self, part of which has gone into the formation of the beloved, whose company shares features of the self engaged in the creative act. Unless these attributes realize the emptiness of a former solitude, they can disrupt what the self has created, for it is not the dominant and/or conscious attributes of the self that are embodied in the beloved, in which case love would be narcissism displaced to a self-image, or the self would be deprived, psychically, of virtual ingredients. In most instances, love arises from unconscious need as a will to bring the self to completion. As in the fable of Aristophanes, the wholeness we are all seeking is a wholeness of unity not a symbiosis or combination.

In love, two halves do not make a whole. Each portion becomes whole by expansion from within. The self generates the other as a complement of, and compensation for, its own inadequacy, such that the self undergoes a growth of its underdeveloped portion. Mind creates, then ingests, its objects even as they externalize. People say of love, without thinking it through, that two become one, but fusion by external contact does not give a whole but an artificial construct, a compilation, a sum, occasional, expedient, as in a companion or the brevity of sexual relations. External

On love

relations can be severed without loss, but internal relations are damaged at the risk of the organism.

∾

What part urge, what part desire? The heart does not choose to fall in love but stills the impulse to say no
One great love ignites a fire that illuminates a cave of isolation
Putting a label on a feeling quells the intensity
Taking a vow compromises the genuine and makes love an obligation
Wit plays with ideas, scoundrels play with feelings
The light from the beloved's eyes comes from the inside, shining to discover what you, yourself, can never know.
The self is not a thing but a category of appearances
Most lovers are enticed by complementary anatomy, a gender incompleteness which, in homosexual love, has to be simulated.
As an expansion of the self, love has no physiognomy.
How can desire, as a category, be fully satisfied by one object?
Those who do not create but acquire a lover will tend to seek others.
I need women so I don't have to relentlessly look for them and can get on with my work. Having a woman keeps me from being distracted by other women.

> If the self is unreal who strives,
> Who lives, loves and dies,
> If not the self within the head
> What is lost when one is dead?

Does love imply its opposite? If so, what is it? Not hate. Perhaps indifference?
If love is the greatest good, indifference is the greatest evil

∾

Rationality in love is like truth in poetry
Without consciousness, is love possible? Would its loss be less painful?
With vivid recall, one ventures into the indefinite.
The tree bare or broken, bent in ice or blossoming,
Is the same in all conditions as a category of itself
I wonder, is a quartet four players or the music divided in parts?
A woman who has to be strenuously wooed is probably not worth having

Those who rely on beauty when young will have nothing left when aging sets in
> Feeling that weakens in objects flourishes in their absence.
> Feeling is a companion that feeds on separation.
> Absence is the garden where loving grows
> The lover's imagination is weakened with sustained outward gaze.
> Why do you ask how much I love you? There are no degrees of loving. Love measured in sacrifice is not a quantity.

> > The road up is the road down:
> > Love for an abstract god,
> > Adoration of a muse
> > Actuality of the beloved

> We had no degrees of separation, no fatuous endearments. I fell into my beloved and almost disappeared
> Love is the beauty of a rose *after* the petals fall off.
> As soon as one begins to judge, love is on the wane.
> I know I love you. There is not a grain of doubt. Do you love me? How can I know? Why should this matter?

> > Drive conceals what wish concedes
> > In love's ideals secured by needs

> No need for longing if the beloved is always with you
> Remember, love is not genuine if a reminder is necessary
> Deceit in lovers is careless appropriation of feeling
> Do not think too deep on love, analysis is the greater peril to instinct and commitment.
> Mystified? Stop thinking and let the thought come to you. I mean, wait for your own thoughts. My words just open a door. Anyway, words are unnecessary. You see the ending in the beginning.
> In a man's gaze, character, in a woman's, soul
> She sees more with a glance than he with a stare
> The best conversation is lovers spouting gibberish.
> There is an intruder at the table, I mean a topic that has come between us.
> Men often succumb to the ether invisible in a woman's silence
> A well-timed remark is worth less than a discreet silence
> The mystery of a woman grows when she declines to respond
> The lies that men tell are no match for a woman's secrets

On love

If it would be narcissistic to love a clone, what about the love between identical twins?

One mourned her best friend,
A canary tweeting to a mirror,
Another re-married two weeks after
The early death of her "great love"
Such shallowness makes one muse
On how it feels to lose
What you never had

Not so comely, not so fair,
She feels a victim to the stare
Of men, victims too of genes and nerves
Blind to virtues, not to curves

When you feel that love is shared
Have you other loves compared
If you still recall the rest
This would be the acid test
Whether lover, friend or wife
Does she matter more than life
If occasion should occur
Would you gladly die for her

The sun sets daily in the west
The moon will rise to reach a crest
One is fire, one is earth
Even more our love is worth
For sun and moon and stars above
Could disappear but not my love

Compassion

Compassion is the idea of love without a beloved

COMPASSION FOR HUMANITY IS a vapid concept. In some sense it is an ideal without an object, or with so many objects the ideal is vacuous. The more that compassion is for the individual, the closer it is to pity, which is more like caring than loving. We grieve for one child killed in an earthquake and shrug off the deaths of thousands. Even the death of two or three individuals dilutes feeling for one. This goes back to the distribution of interest and value over the many and its zeroing-in on the one. The idealization of the one resists that of the many. The value of life takes precedence over humanity, but few take it so far as the Jains. At the other extreme, I have heard highly intelligent Indians advocate a tactical nuclear war with Pakistan to thin the population. It has been said, one death is a tragedy, many a statistic. The hoped-for triumph of Communism for many intellectuals justified the deaths of millions. Perhaps we can begin to love humanity once it takes on value but with so many undeserving, and with boundaries unclear (is a gorilla, a fetus, an imbecile, a person?), for this to happen the other's life must be as precious as your own.

~

Ambition in saint and mystic are sublimated in compassion

Charity in the saint ain't. Dedication for others is to merit god's approval

The blessings of generosity should make gratitude unnecessary

Mortifications in the saintly are preparations for godly visitation

In mystical descent, communion with god passes through an hallucinatory phase. Does the image content disappear and leave god as an unfilled frame?

In the saintly, arrogance is the aggressive pursuit of humility

Compassion

Since arrogance comes of self-importance, the best antidote is indifference

Those with little want a little more. Those with much want much more

A temperate life is recommended, but a life of compromise is unlived

If you feel compassion for others remember, you are dying each moment.

The impossibility of helping everyone should not stop you from helping someone

The tragedy of life is more tragic for some than others.

Those who feel pleasure in the suffering of elevated souls rarely profit from their misfortune.

Some think there is only so much happiness in the world, and that they are deprived by the happiness of others.

To accept suffering is to accept an actuarial fate that is tragic but not a tragedy.

The successful take credit for choices; the rest blame others or bad luck.

> Many women I have met
> More than men, loved their pet
> It is natural, they'd reply
> Birds don't wander like a guy
> Not just for the song it sings
> One can always clip its wings
> Even when there's no affection
> And it tweets at its reflection
> Women learn from tender age
> Keep their birdies in a cage
>
> Who would know another mind
> Or risk it all for what you'll find

Will

*Will carries thought into (as) the world,
which science inserts back into the mind.*

THE ACTIVE QUALITY OF organism, the momentum to forward motion and growth, drive and agency, the life force, can be identified with the Will, the energy or feeling that runs through all living things. Will begins as isotropic or non-directional energy in the inanimate world, passing to the anisotropic or directional feeling that enlivens and empowers the spontaneity of organism, and leads to value in the world, desire and the subjective aim of intentional acts. The variety of manifestations of Will result from the partition and mitigation of force or impulse to wish or desire. Will is not the furnace in the basement that stands behind and fuels an act, but is an intrinsic component at every phase of its development. The dissipation in the strength of Will in the manifold of feelings, from the more intense emotions that reveal the core personality to the subtler affects that characterize its refinement, is only possible if the fractionation of Will occurs together with the individuation of ideas and object-concepts, not as an instigation or motivation or attachment, but ingredient in the specification of a category. In this respect, Will as feeling corresponds to the becoming of an object; being corresponds to the category that becomes what it is.

∞

Will is animal drive that begins in the core and goes out with action. This gives direction to the world.

The strength of Will dissipates when the route to motility diverts to images.

Will as a force that empowers and sustains entails a category of self-preservative behaviors. Desire has a partial category. The category of Will becomes clear when the act or object resolves.

Will

Will takes on a vector as it narrows to desire. The self is a field of limitation.

In drive, the animal is one. In desire, consummation is exchanged for partial intensity.

The plenitude of potential is not a multiplicity of possibilities but a completeness of striving.

The shift of Will from purposefulness to intentionality is the birth of consciousness.

Will—the motive power of thought—is a forward surge, like growth and cognition. There is no reversal, only incomplete renewal.

Impulse and spontaneity are closer to Will than reflection and decision, but Will trickles into all categories and part-acts.

Drive

If we do not feel drive, we are dead already

THE INSTINCTUAL DRIVES—PRIMARILY HUNGER and sexual—that instigate every mental state are the foundation of Will, as an expression of self-preservation and a going-out to the world, and the embodiment of value as the meaning or signification attributed to a given pre-object or path of actualization. Drives are categories of feeling that discharge into acts and objects, or develop to desires. Will is the instinctual empowerment of drive as it fractionates to final acts, while value pertains to a bias in the derivation of feeling as an affective tonality of the pre-object that specifies within a category. Thus, the potential members of the drive of hunger—prey and predation—that fractionate with a quota of affect, if not discharged, develop to sexual drive, in which the ingestion of reproductive material replaces the digestion of food, as copulation with release replaces capture with feeding. If the drive complex is unrealized, it is constrained to desire for a variety of objects in which the pursuit of an absent object replaces the seizure of a present one. One could say hunger reinstates the individual; sexuality does the same through proxy replication, which the maternal instinct serves to guide or insure, while desires are wishes for self-fulfillment that reinforce self-replacement. This is all about the self, its direct or indirect replication and the completion or enhancement of the conscious self-image through others, in love or affection, through experiences or material goods.

∽

The maternal instinct is the post-natal prolongation of the reproductive urge, one planting the seed of a proxy replication, the other nurturing it to separation, i.e. independence.

The organism that dies after reproduction reveals nature's hidden intent

Drive

The force of drive or Will lessens in the progression of drive-based feeling, the lack of implementation and the attenuation of the object-development as the objects of drive-satisfaction diversify to become the aims of desire. Values shift from instinctual need to conscious wish, from replication of the self (in hunger) and replication of the self through progeny (in reproduction) to goals that, though motivated by drives, achieve elaboration and refinement. Hunger and sexuality reproduce the self, which aims at betterment through desire.

Reason begins with instinct and seeks to distance itself from drive, but it is the bias in feeling that carries thought to decision.

If we grow too far from drive, we forget what is truly important in life; love, family.

Consciousness cannot survive without desire; there must be a subjective aim.

The belief in free will saved William James from suicide, but was the instinct for survival or the fear of death a determining factor?

Freud extrapolated the reciprocity of creation and destruction, or arising and perishing, to a death instinct, but perishing is incomplete revival and a necessity for recurrence.

Far from being an instinct, death is an eventuality we cannot avoid. A healthy life is a novel succession of states.

Pleasure and fear of death prolong life after the satisfaction of biological necessity

That death and distraction accompany life and creation does not mean they are instinctual. The world alone is sufficient to kill you without the aid of a drive

The transformation of Will into value is the path of becoming; that from category to object is the path of being

Being is not just what it is, it becomes, while becoming takes on a different quality at each phase in the development of being

Will is instinctive drive as a life force. Value is it's manifestation in object-formation, agency in action. In both, it is the energic property of the self as actor or onlooker Will feels dynamic, value feels static. One is the becoming of self into objects; the other is the object after it becomes what it is.

Feeling and emotion

Without feeling, the self cannot exist.

FEELING RUNS THROUGH ALL mental phases and it is experienced as one with the person, both mind and body. We say, I feel such and such, or I have the feeling that, but especially when the feeling is strong, it pervades the mental state and incorporates the self. The self becomes one with the feeling. Only when feeling is externalized in perception does it objectify as something detached from the self. The transition from desire to object-value carries feeling from mind to world, as the object of desire becomes the value in a desired object.

The non-directional energy in the existence of all entities becomes the directed feeling that enlivens the organic world. This is the vital force (élan vital, Bergson) that animates living things. As feeling deposits drive-energy, it partitions to positive or outgoing, and negative or retreating, trends in behavior. These are the constituents of self-preservation. First, there is hunger (thirst) expressed in feeding and avoiding predation, enabled by aggression and defense. In the satisfaction of hunger, the organism assures its self-replication. The hunger-drive partitions to the sexual-drive, which replicates the organism in surrogates. The primary drive is hunger, then sexuality, with fight and flight, aggression and defense, vectors of drive implementation. The foundational recurrence of all entities evolves in organisms to the replication of self in feeding, and the replication of surrogates in progeny. These constitute the foundational segments of the mind/brain state, determined by instinctual drive.

From this stage, the largely unconscious drive realizes a phase of desire. Basically, with consciousness, the present object of drive is replaced by the absent object of desire. Desire is the specification of precursor phases of drive. The latter are purposeful and directed not to a class of objects (food, mate) but to a singular target, and one that is wished for, not available.

Further, when feeling deposits in drive, it becomes conceptual or categorical. Feeling is not associated to concepts; concepts are not associated to feeling. The concept embraces the feeling, establishes what the feeling is (i.e. en emotion, what it is about, its being) while the feeling is the affect and intensity in the concept, its becoming. Concept and feeling are a unity at the beginning and throughout their development, with fractionation into the variety of emotions and affect-ideas. The enormous range of emotions, from love, hate and fear to grief, despondency, joy, envy, and subtle emotional states, such as shame, humiliation, affection, pride or chagrin, cannot possibly represent different affective qualities. They take on their individuality by the conceptual embodiment of feeling.

The positive and negative directions of drive-implementation individuate into the outward vector of control and the inward vector of timidity. Drive-implementation is initially expressed in aggression and defense, along with the parent drive and in the company of conceptual frames, into the outward vector of control, ambition, greed, exploitation, sadism and so on; and the inward vector of shyness, diffidence, retreat, masochism, compassion, etc. We see this strongly in love and hate, brutality and sacrifice, more subtly in pride and shame, covetousness and generosity, and in the refined emotions which are less oppositional. Conversely, the more intense the emotion, the greater its wholeness and authenticity. States without a discernible object—anxiety, depression—point to the incompleteness or lack of resolution of conceptual-feeling. When the configuration does resolve, emotion changes with consciousness of the object of feeling.

Some writers argue that an inability to think occurs in those rare cases of being unable to feel emotion. However there is no doubt that there would be an inability to feel if thinking should be eradicated, since thought and feeling, concept and affect, are inseparable. Feeling does not inform reason on what to do (Hume); it arises in drive-categories that precede, and are essential to, the occurrence of thought.

∾

I think myself up as a repository of the feeling through which I exist.

We do not usually say, I think that I feel, or I feel that I think, since they are unified

The yin and the yang of the Tao are not opposing states or polarities but vectors of transition.

A simulated mind is an apparition without feeling to give it existence.

The feeling that drives existence is the drive that insures recurrence

In sexual drive, recurrence is insured by proxy replication

Instinct and ancestral urge are truths we can rely upon

The enjoyment of a flower and the existence of a stone; a flood of proto-feeling

Chemotactic systems like crystal structures, not yet organisms, replicate as clones

> Every act of thought
> Refines instinctual drive,
> That from which the self is wrought
> Allows the species to survive

In what sense does feeling exist apart from an object or concept? Feeling and category are unified *ab origo*, passing to supposedly affect-free concepts and concept-free affects, but feeling is inseparable from its conceptual form. The concept identifies the feeling, the feeling gives intentionality and momentum to the concept.

Hard to understand that feeling in existence is more intense for things that do not exist, such as delusions.

Feeling goes out with the object as existence. We know this because objects become thoughts when feeling is withdrawn

Feeling lost in objects returns in objectless states, such as panic

First existence, then interest and value; first distributed over the field, then allotted to particulars.

Energy transposed to feeling imports existence to organism

The direction of feeling completes one cycle of recurrence.

Feeling is the only experience that is not an illusion, partly in the relation to energy, partly because it does not depend on a judgment of truth.

Emotions are eddies in a river of feeling.

One can ask, what do I feel, but this concerns the concept, not the experience.

Intensity of feeling varies with the emotion given by the idea.

Feeling carves objects out of categories as a becoming into being.

An idea is waiting for feeling to bring it to you.

Do not search the thought. Evoke the feeling and the thought will come.

> The world we see is real,
> As real as we feel,
> For every physical kind
> Depends upon the mind.

Wish and Desire

*The conscious desire is that part of unconscious
need that trickles out of fantasy.*

OFTEN WE REALIZE LOVE most intensely when it is lost, when tears of sadness condense like evening dew from a heart that is weeping. Perhaps for some there is consolation in the experience of intensity on the edge of loss, even in despair: "Come then sorrow, sweetest sorrow . . ." Shelley wrote; for those who were loved, or those unloved, or those who never loved, sorrow can be sweet compensation. The loss of a great love is an excision of self, grieving for what is shattered, not just incomplete. The self is ripped in two, leaving an emptiness that can haunt the lover for years. It is one thing to be loved and feel the power that settles inside, but to truly love is to sacrifice the self in an image of one's own making

To be consumed by desire is to be overcome by need.

Desire is for the future. So is a wish, but there is no future in a dream.

The wish is deeper than the desire, the one can be for the impossible, the other closer to the real. This is why the psychoanalyst speaks of unconscious wish. But the unconscious wish is not explicit or specified; it is a result of interpretation of dream events. The wish to kill your father is not ordinarily a conscious desire—much less an act that is carried out—but is extracted from dream images or the meanings assigned to symbols. Unlike desire, unconscious wish is not intentional, which requires agency. In dream, the self is passive to the subjective aim. Moreover, a wish requires a self that wishes. In dream, the wish is postulated before the event. That is, there is only the dream event. Wishing and a self that wishes are inferred.

Thus, a dream about the death (murder) of a man (father) can be interpreted as the wish of the dreamer, but without agency the dream self is not culpable. Even if the dreamer is, in the dream, a part of the action, the dream self is passive to the events such that the killing is open to interpretation.

Oedipus did not wish to kill his father, and was jolted by the discovery. The "cides"—homi/sui/fratri/matri/patri/infanti—have been with us since the dawn of human time. Most often this drama of life is played out in the confines or context of family. What makes these unconscious wishes? Should we assume that Sophocles was inspired by the unconscious idea that Freud made famous? A literary work, even one that is autobiographical or self-referential, has the latitude to incorporate fantasies, some conscious, others unconscious or unintended, that for one reason or another never materialize. Could one say the unconscious wish ignites the unactualized potential behind a conscious desire?

Desire is for an absent or anticipated object or event, generally within the realm of possibility, though the line between fantasy and objectivity is vague. In conscious desire, the self wants something. In unconscious wish, there is no evidence of wanting, and an indefinite relation of the self to the supposed wish.

Another interpretation, more biological, might be the impulse of the child to attract all the attention of the mother so as to limit the possibility of an impregnation that would lead to competition for resources—milk, food, protection—much as firstborns of many species will kill the siblings that are born later. Rather than sex with the mother, the mandate is to block access to her by competing males. This would help to explain sibling rivalry.

The unconscious wish is not the consciously "hoped-for"—indeed, it is generally denied—while the object of the wish is rarely explicit in the dream. There is no hoping, no expectation, no uncertainty or future possibility. In the dream, what happens is happening now. It is a dubious argument that dreams are wishes, or wish-fulfillments, for most dreams have little to do with wishes. Some are banal, like going to the market, others are frightening and many are distortions of memories. Most dreams are conditioned by day residues, often the least noticed events, or by cultural and social factors, or by the analyst's bias. They involve events in the distant past, persons long dead, and are often fantasies beyond possibility. Dreams can incorporate sounds, such as an alarm clock as a church bell. They solve problems.

In dream, events devour the self as a target, not an instigator. In unconscious wish, something happens, and the self is accused of wanting it, albeit in fantasy or symbolism. One can wish certain individuals would die, one can love them, hate them or have ambivalence. The death of the father assumes more importance, in myth and in psychoanalysis. The centrality of the oedipal theme to analytic work is due to the proximity and contact with family; it is not an encapsulated scenario that recurs of necessity in every family setting. The point is, the family is a tinder box, ground zero, for the loves, hates and jealousies that will be enacted later in the world.

The primary drive is to autonomy. The trend to individuation may cause friction but is not a murderous wish. Tension is not, I would argue, necessarily related to gender but to separation from the dominant parent. If the mother is dominant, one has Adlerian anger; if the father, perhaps features of oedipal conflict. The mother (breast) is the subjective world of the newborn (Mahler) as intra-personal space expands to an extra-personal component. Gradually, objects articulate the extra-personal, which finally detaches as an extra-psychic (mind-independent)—but still subjective—space. Concurrently, the intra-psychic is specified by images, ideas, feelings and the self. The individuation process entails a residue of tension as autonomy is realized out of belongingness. This is not a conflict of ancestral themes or psychic homunculi but the fractionation of an individuality that is striving to separate from the family structure.

～

Is the self the wish or the act? Suppose you want to strangle your boss after a hard day at work but have "second thoughts". Is the boss an authority figure or does he represent someone else? And who is the "real" you, the self of the wish or the self of restraint?

Is every father authoritative, is any male a father-figure? Is Freud's emphasis on the son-father relation a result of the absence of his own father and a consequently greater intimacy with his mother? In a word, have we all inherited the neurotic element in Freud's personality?

If the wish develops when value fails to suppress it, what is the self without fear of censure or punishment, and only the influence of core values?

The wish is intrinsic; the constraints are often extrinsic, penalty or reward.

We say, careful what you wish for, but the adage should be, careful how an unconscious wish is interpreted.

What works of literary imagination point to unconscious wish? Does the work inform a theory, or does a theory select the work?

Images in unconscious thought follow laws of metaphor and similar relations, not the conscious narrative that strings them together.

Occasionally, a lovely phrase comes to me fully formed and only after a while do I realize that it makes no sense. Or, did the sense escape me?

An image or event appears in dream. The wishful nature of the event is inferred. What makes it a wish if the self does not wish it?

Anything can represent a wish, or a fear the wish will come to pass, and anything can have a symbolic reference. The blinded Oedipus does not want to see what he has done. The lame Oedipus could represent impotence. In the myth, the outcome of fate –an oracular prophecy—plays the part of unconscious necessity.

Some have proposed that nightmares are sexual panics (Jones). This is illustrated in the Fusilli painting with one element of the nightmare, suffocation, shown by an incubus sitting on a voluptuous woman who is supine in bed; it is claimed that nightmares in men occur mainly in the prone position. If these are also repressed sexual wishes, one might think they would be more common in sexually repressed societies.

As a young man, I had a nightmare in which I was skin-diving and my leg was trapped in the mouth of a giant clam. I thought I was drowning and woke in a sweat. I suppose the analyst would say that my phallic leg, my wet foot (Oedipus), was locked in union with the gaping vagina of an oceanic hermaphrodite. Or, did the dream condense some life-threatening adventures that occurred spear-fishing at a great depth off the California coast?

There are many species that devour their young but few the reverse. The myth of Cronos who ate his sons is more in keeping with the biological tendency than that of Oedipus, though it does lay down the rationale for retaliation or proactive patricide.

It is dispiriting that generosity to children breeds a sense of entitlement, with bitterness to follow should it be suspended.

Gratitude is most genuine as a sacrifice of the giver. Otherwise, however much is given it is never enough.

Common struggle forges a stronger bond than kindness or indulgence.

The genius is often raised by a strong woman with an absent father (e.g. Sartre, Freud). Does the creative take the place of mundane resentment?

Love is immune to rational judgment, which justifies a tacit or non-rational bias. Even a rational compass has limitations.

Equality hopes to mitigate disparity in deference to reason, but the erotic is aroused by imbalance.

When a great love is lost, mourning is no substitute. The heart that is crushed wants to go with the beloved.

Wish and Desire

    Sexual pleasure in surrender is a sign that submission is essential

    I thought she was mine; then I realized I was a victim of my own seduction

    Be aware, forgiveness may be merciful but it is the key to enslavement

    In love, pleasing gives pleasure. If you do not feel this, perhaps you are deceived

> She doesn't jog, she jiggles,
> She doesn't walk, she wiggles,
> So many moving parts
> Wherever loving starts

> Oh my dear, what you ask,
> No man could refuse
> But no gentleman could accept

    She wears her body as an ornament, expecting men to ignore it and focus on the genuine, as if a fish that swallows the bait should love the frying pan

> Though not among my fears,
> Nor little did I note
> In the Talmud, she wrote,
> God counts a woman's tears

> Young girls compile a list to find the perfect mate
> They fail to find the man they want and soon accommodate

> Oh, the girls of yesteryear
> Before the men, filled with fear,
> Afraid if they approached too near
> Their livelihood would disappear

> When Arthur Koestler died,
> His lover, young with many years ahead,
> Chose suicide instead

> Zeno stubbed his little finger
> And decided not to linger

The couple played the lottery over twenty long years hoping to win enough to finally afford divorce

When love slips away, guilt is not a tactic but an insidious attack on self-empowerment

> Infidelity divides the whole
> From two to three in the soul
> For each beloved less remains
> As feeling divvies up the gains

> Love like personality, can survive an injury.
> Passion, like inebriation, wears off in the morning

Adultery for the unadventurous is an exotic vacation, though travel may be less costly

Suspicious of your mate? Choose stability or risk interrogation

Can love remain strong if the wise overlook what the naïve deplore?

The skin quivers with expectation, there is nothing I can say, every act is uncertain, how to walk, how to breathe, a torrent of embarrassed tears, a tree, a child's face, I am incapacitated, vulnerable, yet at that moment most alive

> Every man must correctly guess
> If a maybe is a yes
> But when a no becomes a maybe
> And he starts to call you baby
> Better tell him no is no
> So he knows how far to go

> Think about a past event
> How it felt, what it meant
> Ideas in mind come and go
> Pictures in a picture show
> Stripped of feeling felt back then
> Never felt the same again
> So let me dream of you tonight
> Shield you darkly from the light
> Sense the old intensity
> That waking does not come to me

Wish and Desire

Though our love remains alive
In reveries that you revive
Ever fresh without decay
Recalling melts the pain away

Asceticism

One can be a half-hearted ascetic without going whole hog.

WHY DO MOST PEOPLE seek to acquire and enjoy all the riches of life while others— denouncing it as a life of indulgence or hedonism— choose a path of self-denial? For the religious, it may be to appear worthy for union with god. For others, it is to share or donate abundance. Still others seek self-discipline to avoid distraction from what, to them, matters more in life. Whether it be devotion to a cause, philosophical or creative work, the common theme is a rejection of the adventitious for the sake of the essential. In the extreme, all common pleasures and comforts of life are conceived as ornamental, to be stripped away to bare subsistence, presumably under the spell of an idea so compelling that it replaces the need for all diversions.

A rejection of the outer world of enjoyments and frivolities accompanies a strict code of austerities that rigidly disavows all but what is necessary to survival. In most instances, this is not in the service of creative thought but for personal redemption or salvation, or a search for deeper insight or knowledge, oneness with god or nature, purification, or the recapturing of a primeval state. However, in all instances, whether the eccentric practices of a Sadhu or the single-minded dedication of a philosopher or scientist, they are guided, or misguided, by a search for some truth that is elusive to those who are captive to passing attractions. This goal justifies or compensates for a commitment to a life of deprivation. From a psychological perspective, the question is how can an idea take over a person such that the bare satisfactions are sufficient to enable an ascetic to gaze unswervingly at the aim?

The similarity with obsession is obvious but there is no clear relation between a recurrent focus and an exclusion of other experiences. If asceticism is obsession, it spills over into all aspects of thought and behavior. One can have an obsessive love but still not eliminate other human needs and desires. Indeed, if a person became an ascetic due to obsessional love, it is likely the object of this love would lose interest—not that this would matter—for the obsession to continue. Moreover, an obsession usually has a focus, or foci, while the aim of the ascetic is transcendental, an experience of god, the Absolute, the purpose of life, and so on. In obsession, there is no reward, whereas for the ascetic, a denial of the amenities of life brings him closer to a subjective aim that is stronger for being unclothed of irrelevant apparel.

The diverse motivations for the ascetic life share the preeminence of one idea or category of thought to the exclusion of all others. This intense focus is brought on by the denial of ordinary comforts and pleasures. The elimination of thought and behavior that might deter the individual from an absolute focus, regardless of the nature of the guiding idea, is an extreme accentuation of the usual process through which ideas or trends in thought arise in consciousness, differing only in the pervasiveness of the idea. It is the generality to all aspects of behavior, and the benefits that self-denial supposedly brings that drive the individual. Certainly the justification must be strong, or the pleasure in abject poverty and simplicity of life so agreeable, or the rewards so enormous, as to sacrifice a life for a quest that is illusionary and usually quixotic.

There is commonly a relation to mysticism that enhances denial such as suffering, mortification, penury, bodily neglect or abuse, solitude, subduing the flesh in search of the deeper, hidden meaning or enlightenment that is inaccessible to a mind cluttered with worldly affairs. The nature of enlightenment is unclear since it is ineffable, though presumably there is an immediacy of contact with deity, emptiness, the ground of existence, uncovered in layers of descent to the intra-psychic nucleus of mind. Those who appear to experience enlightenment are unable to communicate the feeling to others.

In the mystical state, the shift from mind-external to mind-internal does not stop with thought and imagination. The ordinary concepts of thought are products of desire or expectation left aside for an antecedent category—that of creation, spirit or generativity—out of which the appetites and part-concepts fractionate. The deeper the withdrawal, the more the originating category replaces its successors, even to a phase prior to word-selection. The goal is to achieve a unity with a primal phase in mind that gives birth to concepts and the renunciation of the objects into which they distribute. The category is not so much transcendental as generative—the seed of life, interpreted as god, the ground of existence, the spiritual core of mind and world. To become one with this phase, if only once and then briefly, is to feel the secret knowledge that is given to those who earn it by abandoning the fragmentary objects it deposits. The categorical prime of drive is reconfigured as the spiritual progenitor of being. For the ascetic in a mystical state, who retreats to the core of mind, the generative power of drive, which embraces all subsequent derivations—concepts, things, events—retains its force as diffuse feeling that is unified in the loss of directionality. In the absence of subjective aim, the elimination of objects and vectors, the outcomes of drive-realization are relinquished.

∽

Psychoanalysis also withdraws to earlier phases in mind through free association and dream-report, but mystical descent goes deeper.

The danger in a prolonged descent is permanent detachment.

Enlightenment or mystical intuition is feeling, not knowledge. As with love, we want to feel the experience even if we have an idea of what it is like.

I suppose the question can be asked: is a brief feeling of oneness, intuition, or a sense of the affective ground of truth, worth a lifetime of preparation?

The more restrictive, narrow, encapsulated or eccentric the routine of an ascetic, the less involvement with non-communal others, the hermitic isolation or support of like-minded groups, the less temptation there is to distraction.

To feel spirit in the world is not necessarily to believe in a spiritual world but to feel reverence for what is beyond comprehension.

The mystical inhabits the unsaid in a logical statement or true proposition. We see this in the four-pronged logic of Buddhism.

Think: A, A and not-A, neither A nor not-A, both A and not-A. Are there other possibilities?

> All things perish to exist
> Die in time to timeless be
> Nothing can in time persist
> Without a brief eternity
>
> The net of Indra casts a spell
> Upon the vibrant strings
> Throbbing parts inside that dwell
> A multiplicity of things

Asceticism

Motion is in everything
In whole and in the parts
Each concrete thing is perishing,
Before the next one starts

Moderation in everything is rational but adventure is at the extremes.

Water cleaves with icy waves
Before the freeze the heron flew
Souls that sleep in silent graves,
Dreaming of the summer dew

Look around and listen well,
Roots that cling to sod and soil,
Pulsing through organic fields
With nature birthing all in all

Oh blade of grass, Oh shadowing tree,
The greatest or the least unknown,
All perish without enmity,
Life to life through death is sown

Sense devolves from things diverse
To purpose in the mental stream
To see within the universe
More than what at first may seem

Hedonism

Deep felt enjoyment is at risk in hedonic excess, which attempts to regain in diversity what is lost in satisfaction.

IN SOME RESPECTS, HEDONISM would seem the opposite of asceticism. Thus, at one extreme the ascetic leaves the external world for inner mind and the hope of achieving a state of transcendence. At the other, the hedonist dives into a world of pleasure (and avoidance of displeasure) in a diversity of amusements. For the ascetic, the sought-for experience may involve a lifetime of renunciation; for the hedonic, there is no mystery to be realized but much to be gained in ephemeral pleasures. One would say they inhabit opposing polarities in the mental state, one the core, the other its derivation into the world, but there are other important differences. For one thing, asceticism has a spiritual motivation while hedonism is a natural behavior that tends to be explained by a principle of pleasure associated with human nature. The hedonist enjoys what the ascetic denies. Hedonism is constrained by values, law, opportunity and the direction and magnitude of appetite, while ascetic practice is essentially unconstrained except by a personal belief system.

While the ascetic may pass a life of deprivation without achieving enlightenment, even a moderate hedonist can reflect on the pleasurable experiences of life, especially those of love, family and other gratifications. Whether or not the quest for pleasure brings happiness or ephemeral satisfaction is compensation enough for the lack of transcendental insight. The ascetic has a life of mortification, deprivation and/or suffering with no guarantee of spiritual awakening or mystical insight though it brings him closer to the intrapsychic sources of mind, while hedonic pleasure, in the extreme, can fritter a life away in senseless enjoyment, avoiding seriousness of thought, purpose, commitment and the realm of spirit. Hedonism can

Hedonism

be selfish or generous, profligate or disciplined. One can love with devotion or orgy all night, eat voraciously like an animal or with the delicacy of a gourmet. The ascetic can live naked in a cave or have a social life with modest needs. It seems largely a matter of the degree of inwardness or extroversion. The hedonist may feel his life—or life generally—is meaningless, and is skeptical as to the legitimacy of the ascetic way of life. He may see asceticism as futile and deliberate disengagement with life, without possibility of attaining a transcendent experience, which is probably delusional. The only purpose in life is to survive and prosper, which for the hedonic temperament is taken to mean "gather ye rosebuds while ye may," whether as a pastime or a career.

∾

If there is a spiritual aspect in hedonism, it is when one truly loves beauty.

Refinement is compatible with hedonic desire in the choice of objects. It is a matter of taste. One can binge on cheap wine or a rare Bordeaux.

We speak of physical and emotional pain, but grief and sorrow have nothing in common with a toothache. Animals feel pain, even lower forms, but what is animal pleasure?

Drugs to mitigate pain also give pleasure. The pain avoids addiction by soaking up narcotics.

In frontal lobotomy, pain is felt without a painful quality. What is this like?

Stimulation of brain areas gives pleasure without an object—the so-called pleasure centers. Pleasure can be induced by many events, but while the events differ, the pleasure in each category is much the same.

Are "pleasure centers" activated by meals, poetry, aesthetic enjoyment, a walk in the country, nostalgia, or do these different events have an affective tone that varies with their objects and effects?

If sexual pleasure is the most intense, are other pleasures milder degrees? Does sexual drive fractionate to diverse pleasures, or is a reservoir of pleasure aroused by different events?

Pain *on* the body is referred to the body part; *in* the body, it has a locus but no object. We can locate a pain with some precision but pleasure is a generalized bodily feeling that is referred to events rather than objects.

When a person gives pleasure, it is the receiving, not the giving, to which the pleasure is referred.

Pleasure and the avoidance of displeasure trace back to the positive and negative vectors of instinctual drive; fight and flight, aggression and defense.

We have pleasure in remembrance but cannot revive a feeling of pain.

A painful memory is a metaphor. What we mean is the memory of an unhappy experience.

Some children cannot feel pain. There is a congenital absence of certain neurons. I described such a case. Are there people who cannot feel pleasure?

I studied a woman with a small stroke in the brainstem who was distraught that when she felt sad she could no longer cry.

Pleasure is internal but usually it needs provocation. I doubt the pleasure in a symphony differed for Beethoven after he became deaf. Reading a musical score is like reading poetry.

Unlike deprivation, pleasure can be addictive; the addiction is to reproduce the pleasure.

The opposite of pain is anesthesia, not pleasure

Some degree of asceticism comes in the course of life as little by little pleasures disappear. One can go from hedonism to asceticism simply by waiting until you tire of life. This may lead to wisdom but not enlightenment.

Greater pleasure is extracted from one event than many. Listening to Robert Merrill singing "*il balen*" gives me more pleasure than many nights at the opera.

The more narrow the focus of worldly pleasures, the greater the intensity. The feeling that distributes into the many coalesces into the one.

Pain and pleasure are feelings that provide reasons for a behavior, not arguments on its behalf.

Far from being a philosophy of life, hedonism is a flight from thought. The connoisseur who makes a philosophy of taste elevates experience and sensibility to an art.

The suppression of desire in the ascetic and its liberation in the hedonic; but what changes a desire other than a desire to change?

What happens to the desire to give up all desires?

I do not think pleasure turns into pain, though tickling to excess, which involves pain fibers, can give displeasure. In contrast, pain often gives pleasure, especially when it is sexual or masochistic. This is usually explained by postulating something else, such as low self-esteem, without addressing the pain/pleasure relation.

The pain-pleasure dichotomy is an extension of the +/- variable in all life forms. A paramecium will approach a soft light and avoid a bright one.

This takes one variable from the manifold of behavior as an explanation of its richness.

The self is articulated by objects in the hedonic and unified by their absence in the ascetic.

Narcissism

I tend to think someone is a narcissist if they have no interest in me. Does this make me a narcissist as well?

THERE ARE DIFFERENT WAYS of thinking about narcissism. The first is in relation to arrogance, ambitiousness and/or intolerance of others. This form of narcissism confuses self-love with an excess of the instinctual hunger and aggression that gives rise to greed and self-serving or egocentric behavior. Many psychologists would say such behavior is a compensation for inadequacy or low self-esteem, not self-love. Another description might include those who are selfish, self-absorbed and indifferent to the needs of others. But lack of interest, sympathy or concern for others does not readily translate to love of self. The miserly temperament may be filled with self-hate, which becomes a misanthropic sentiment.

From a philosophical perspective, the narcissist is a functional solipsist who is the all and center of his world. The disdain for others is closer to indifference for those in an external world that has a kind of imaginary status, serving less as an object of signification than as a means of self-pleasure. As in the myth, Narcissus gazes at his reflection until he dies, a fitting metaphor for the illusory quality of objects, the self-creation of the beloved and the detachment from a world of appearance.

Love is the creation of a beloved by the self, a beloved who embodies the needs and feelings of the self, whether identical to the self or its compliment. The image of the other can be self-sufficient, not a reflection of the lover except to fill an absence. The lover can be said to love an image created by the self which could be externalized in the form of romantic love; mirrored like the myth or as an internal receptacle for feelings that might otherwise flow into a beloved or other objects. For Narcissus, the world has essentially vanished; all that is left is a mirror image of the outer manifestation of the self, with existence a bubble of an inner self gazing on appearance. The object field distills to the self or the beloved, as feeling saturates the image without distributing into other objects.

Now, images can externalize as hallucinations or as objects, and thoughts can externalize in psychotics, but the self can also externalize in the rare condition of autoscopy in which there is a brief image of the self, a *Doppelgänger*. This was described in the poem by Heine, and the Schubert song in which the image of the beloved is replaced by the image of the self.

∾

Du Doppelgänger! du bleicher Geselle!
Was äffst du nach mein Liebesleid,

Ordinarily, those we describe as narcissists have an exaggerated sense of self-importance, especially as to beauty and intelligence, usually at the expense of, or with indifference to, others. The emphasis on beauty, with conceit and vanity, is too common to mention, but the lack of modesty concerning intelligence, no less common, is an attribute of many academics, a prized commodity that leads them to denigrate and bicker, acting like peacocks to an obliging public or to offend colleagues and acquaintances who, oblivious to their own narcissistic tendencies, endure their insufferable pretensions.

Does the category of the self receive or retain the feeling that would ordinarily go into a multitude of derivations? Or are certain features of the self, such as beauty and intelligence, weighted with affect at the cost of less flattering attributes, either of the self or of other people? In the imaginative reconstruction of this theme in Oscar Wilde's *Dorian Gray*, the mirror likeness is a canvas that undergoes aging, while the self remains youthful and hedonistic. Here, in a reversal of the Narcissus myth, the Doppelgänger ages like any person while the idealized self does not grow old. The reversal also points to the difference between a love that is devoted to the other, or to an image of the self, and the individuation—thus, the diminution—of feeling into many objects of loveless pleasure. These accounts of the narcissistic personality, whether an objectification of the self, a hallucination, a painting or a mirror image, and the relation of self-love to romantic love, and by implication the feeling given to or withdrawn from other objects, point to a world of appearance with an affective intensity concentrated on an inner or outer realization of the self, as feeling retracts from the object field and decants into one image of inestimable value.

Some say, love yourself before you love others, but this is just an immunization against the possibility of loss.

Can narcissists love those who do not feed their narcissism?

We don't say, first you must hate, envy or fear yourself, so why do we say love yourself? Perhaps this means be confident, assured and comfortable, but love requires vulnerability.

Cynics say narcissism is the only love that lasts but how can the self be both agent and recipient?

Can narcissism develop out of disinterest in others, or neglect of personal deficiencies; that is, does an absence of critical self-judgment give narcissism by default?

The narcissist lacks genuine interest in others, but a lack of such interest does not imply narcissism.

The pursuit of self-interest can be dedication. What matters is if the person feels more important than the objects of interest.

Chimpanzees show self-recognition in a mirror. In some cases of dementia this ability can be selectively lost, along with an alteration of mirror space. Does the chimp have a self-concept? Does the demented person lose it?

Some nomads in the desert may never see their reflection. How would this affect the self-concept? How much of the self depends on what one looks like?

If I had no idea of my appearance, my face and body, would I still have the same self-concept? Would a brain-in-a-vat have a self? One wants to believe this would be so since it occurs in dream, but I'm not sure.

What happens to the self in someone paralyzed from the neck down, basically a voice without bodily feeling?

Love for others comes and goes but can one stop loving one's self? What would cause this and what would it be like?

> Sometimes I wonder what you'd do
> If you loved me as I love you
> If I found a new caress
> Would you want my happiness
> Instead of rage and jealousy
> Were I your friend and you loved me
>
> Did I see within her eyes
> The spark of love or compromise

Illusion and conviction

To know that mind is illusory is one thing. To feel it, another.
The difference is like that of certainty and conviction.

THE SKEPTICAL WORM IN the apple of conviction is the illusory quality of all mental phenomena. It plants a seed of doubt in every feeling, idea and experience, and introduces a conceptual ingredient in every demonstration of fact. In the case of conviction, a person's faith or absolute belief, however unrealistic or powerful, is open to question by others. For those with strong conviction, whether religious, political or experiential, the belief is almost unshakeable. Indeed, to abandon such a conviction is close to a religious conversion, even if the beliefs are judged to be nonsense by critical others, whose judgment, no matter how informed and impartial, is no less vulnerable to skepticism. In the sphere of emotion, which accompanies conviction, the instability of feeling is "contained" by the category or ideal to which it is "attached". The first crack in the armor of conviction is a wavering of the affective tone, the dynamic within the idea that makes the belief unshakeable. An idea can be challenged and refuted, but it is the affective intensity that makes the idea resistant to argument. Conviction can also be mitigated by uncertainty but more likely the initial change is a lessening of emotional resolve.

The conviction in most beliefs is not fully rational. In fact, such beliefs are often delusional. One could say an illusion in perception becomes a delusion in belief. While the illusory nature of belief, as with other mental states, should make one less absolutist concerning their truth, opinions on deeply held beliefs carry such conviction it is nearly impossible to persuade someone of their fraudulence or uncertainty. Given that mind is phenomenal, every fact is potentially false and every truth has the possibility of refutation. There is no certain knowledge, only degrees of approximation to the real, that is, the closeness to which thought and perception map to reality, or what is inferred from the accuracy of this correlation for and across individuals. The validity, reliability or truth of a mental state is determined by the pragmatic utility, the adaptive value or efficacy of the underlying belief. Since every act or demonstration is a psychic phenomenon, there is inevitably some error in representation, so that it is impossible to have absolute knowledge of external reality. Except in closed systems such as mathematics or redundant propositions, the only timeless truth is that there is no timeless truth.

Considering the evolutionary advancement of thought, and the gradations of untrustworthiness of its realizations, it is striking how rapidly conviction can form, usually independent of falsification, verification or evidence for or against the belief. A person can be converted to a suicidal terrorist in a matter of weeks, even days. A conviction for alternative medicine or a vegetarian diet can be (pun aside) all-consuming. The belief in the coming devastation of global warming—justified or not—can take over a life even when the person knows little or nothing of the technical data, has no training or skill in the science, and relies on the internet for information that reinforces a predisposition. There is no critical appraisal of opposing views, no ability to question the controlling belief, and often an impulse to propagandize or convert others. Political opinions on diverse topics tend to be held with such conviction that non-believers are denigrated and ridiculed. How is it that people so impassioned are immune to rational discourse, unable to engage in critical discussion or entertain other perspectives? Especially since, as discussed, all beliefs are open to question and past occurrences will be interpreted to fit an agenda or ongoing narrative, such as a 9/11 conspiracy, though most such beliefs concern future outcomes that are unpredictable, even improbable?

One possibility is that the need for conviction does not follow argument but seeks opportunities for satisfaction, whether religious, political, a cult and so on. This implies discontent with a formerly uncommitted self, or an intense but undischarged quota of affect in the category of the self-concept that presses to actualization. The drive-based hunger for a category of belief resonates with needs and the conceptual-feeling that allows the belief to actualize in an emotional idea—the conviction. Because the category overlaps with the self-concept, it is a major part of the sense of identity. The stronger the conviction, the more it resembles delusion, and the more it defines the self, from an intra-personal point of view. This is why uncertainty as to the belief, or receptiveness to disputation, can threaten the very ground of the self and the core of an illusory personhood.

Regardless of whether the belief is true or not, a person in the grip of an unshakeable conviction exhibits features of delusion. What is the difference in the psychotic with command hallucinations from god or the devil instructing him to kill someone, and Abraham, who was similarly instructed by god to sacrifice his son? In one, the pathology is widespread and the belief is a part of a larger delusional system; in the other it is restricted to one act or category. However, from the standpoint of the category and psychological perspective, neither the justification in one instance to kill a sinner, nor in the other to prove worthy of god's love or to test one's faith is sufficient for a distinction. Both are delusions accompanied by the hallucination of a voice, in which an other-worldly image passes to conviction in an illogical and dangerous belief.

Hallucination is a mental image that replaces an object and persists with the eyes closed as in dream whereas an illusion, such as a rainbow, is a distortion of perception that disappears on closure of the eyes. An illusion can also be described as a non-veridical or mistaken perception, or the erroneous interpretation of perceptual experience, which applies to most forms of false belief. With an expansion in the psychic distance between an object and a false or misconstrued perception, the perception becomes hallucinatory.

An illusion or hallucination is judged to be unreal by comparison to external objects. Without this comparison, the illusion is taken for reality. Conversely, objects are judged to be real by comparison to illusions or dreams. But objects can be judged as unreal in comparison to the physical reality which they model. The belief in the reality of objects is due, on the one hand, to a comparison with dream and imagery; and on the other, to a lack of direct knowledge of the physical world. Without a comparison to something beyond an object, the object is all there is.

At this point, we tend to diagnose a pathological state, even though this is precisely what happens during mystical trance in the feeling of a direct communion with god. In ordinary states of conviction, a person under the spell of an illusion shows a greater or lesser departure from fact or veracity. Experience is misinterpreted, de-contextualized and/or exaggerated, and usurps other attributes of personality. The intensity of belief outweighs the evidence, or the belief does not admit to possible error. What is fascinating about the formation of conviction is the degree of emotional investment. Unlike the certainty of science or the conclusions of a philosophical argument, in which truth is provisional, there is an exclusion of the possibility of error. Thus, the question is why the affective component of the belief-category becomes so intense that the idea is impenetrable to disconfirmation, even mitigation. Presumably, feeling is allocated—or diverted—to the belief-category—religious, political, other—at the cost of an investment in other ideas. The need for commitment and its outcome in identification shore up the sense of self. Conviction for a category of ideas comes to define the goals and purpose of a life. The belief is not a property of the self; it is not something the self has or possesses. Rather, in the overlap, even the replacement of the self, the self is driven by the belief-category. Put differently, the self of conviction is not the owner of the belief but its manifestation.

The allocation of feeling to a belief, and the part it plays in the self, are similar to what happens in passionate love, which also has features of delusion. In love, feeling concentrates in the category (ideal) of the beloved. The lover cannot be dissuaded from a conviction in the value of the beloved, much as occurs with an idea, a faith or cause. As the ideal of the beloved is an illusion, as the conviction in love approaches delusion, as love consumes the individual and dominates the self, the individual sacrifices for the other or ideal whether one falls in love slowly or rapidly. The similarities with religious and political conviction become evident, which also involve affectively-charged ideals that can form gradually, over a brief period or at first sight. In love, feeling flows into an idealized category, the beloved; in other forms of conviction, feeling is bound less to a specific individual than to a category of ideas or an idealized goal in which exemplifications satisfy the category.

This resemblance demonstrates the continuity across disparate forms of belief and feeling and the illusory ideals of their objects, as well as the relation of illusion to conviction, and the transition from ordinary beliefs to pathological conditions. A single process of actualization leading from core belief and the unconscious self to objects in the world, influenced at various points in the path to realization, determines the manifestations of the belief, the intensity of feeling and the degree of conviction. The concentration of feeling turns an idea into an ideal that justifies the conviction, which intensifies and weakens when feeling partitions into many lovers or many ideas. Devotion to the beloved, to god, to a social movement, differ in their individuations, but all have the same source, the same conviction, the same intensity of feeling, and the same illusory ideal. The delusional quality of conviction becomes pathological when the belief is incoherent and deviates markedly from reality or consensual faith. Conviction in love does not need the support of others but requires reciprocity from the beloved. Conviction in politics, lacking reciprocity, needs reinforcement by others. Love can become delusional when it is penetrated by jealousy, paranoia, suspiciousness, erotomania and so on. Religious faith entails the love of or for a god, while conviction in political belief becomes love in the devotion to a leader.

∾

The intense feeling of conviction can be a force for good or evil, love or hate, or some mixture depending on the contribution of instinctual aggression or defense.

Conviction in love excludes the world; in faith or politics, it seeks to change the world. In one, the ideal of the beloved is the subjective aim; in the other, the multiple objects of the belief-category carry conviction into the world.

The variety of acts in the name of conviction is justified by the dedication to an idealized category (beloved, god, social good).

The intensity of conviction specifies the category that shares in the self-concept.

The self that is open to conviction closes once it takes root.

As in love, it is nearly impossible to have more than one deep conviction. In love there is one object, in conviction there are many.

Conviction is not certainty. One is absolute, emotive; the other reasonable, open to question. Conviction usurps the feeling that is excluded in rational judgment.

God

Why single out the belief in god for denial when you are in such a state of delusion? It might be the only true belief you have.

THE PROGRESSIVE LOSS OF the spiritual in nature parallels the ascent of materialist doctrine in science. The gods of animism that inhabit mind-external devolve to local deities—the Pantheon of the Greeks, the myriad gods of the Hindus. The population of spirits in nature declines along with the diversity of faculties in mind, which are gradually replaced by chips and circuit boards as the mind becomes a machine. The reduction of organism to the physical and the expulsion of spirit from physical nature correspond to the abolition of consciousness from a computer brain. The materialism of a mechanical world of causal interaction accompanies causal relations among components in a robot. For brain as a computational network, individuals are automata.

In evolutionary theory, god is unnecessary. The mind is reduced to inputs, outputs, buffers and central processors and thought is causal and contingent. The relation of god to nature is comparable to the relation of mind to brain. If we understood how self and thought arose from the physical matter of brain, we would understand the relation of god or spirit to physical nature. The insolubility of the god/nature problem has resulted in a wide scale secularism that affects all aspects of society and science, along with an effort to eliminate the mind/brain problem. Mind is collapsed to brain without remainder, and without an explanation of how it arises. Reduction is an expedient that works in only one direction.

There is probably a grain of truth in Freud's claim that the near-universal belief in god fulfills the need for an all-powerful, all-knowing, all-loving and all-merciful paternal figure. However, there is little actual evidence for this supposed need, whether it is in those who are believers or atheists, or in those with or without a good father. I think it more likely that properties of the human mental state predispose to this belief. First, there is the subjectivity of external space—a continuous sheet of mind into every niche of perceptible nature—which condenses to a spirit world of gods, demons, totems, and magical or supernatural thought. Then there is the pervasive drive to meaning, which appears in all aspects of thought, and is especially prominent in animism. Finally, there is the pattern of derivation of the mental state, which goes from depth to surface. This leads to the idea of god as a finality, an ultimate, a higher, superior, celestial being.

You believe your wife loves you, that your work is important, that your life has meaning and purpose, that the politician you vote for wants to improve your life. You know from an objective standpoint that you are dust in the universe but you can't believe that either. You are anxious when you are ill. Do you expect to live forever?

∽

Apart from Pascal's wager, why not believe in god's existence? Most other beliefs you hold are false

You look in the wrong place if you seek god outside

If the timelessness of deity is not in the temporal world, dissolve to mind-internal to sense eternity in god

> God is not beyond the whole
> But deep within the believing soul

God and nature are one in descent beneath the floor

The oneness of the mystic with god is not out-there in the world of astrophysics, or buried in the vibrations of superstrings, but in the core of mind-internal

There is small comfort in a god of creative advance. Yet the forward surge uplifts human mind, and a god of change offers hope of renewal.

Leaving mind-external for union with an interior god is a state ineffable but real

Not in the evening sky or in heaven beyond the stars, or in every molecule or the vast diversity of astounding nature

An expansion in meditation of the momentary present as part of the eternal now of god is a deception inside an illusion.

If we all arise from the same root, petals on a tree of life, synchronicity is possible.

A god of change within nature, at one with natural process, infuses all things with spirit. This is a god that lives within us, as in every entity, as with Indra's net in the Buddha-nature. Such a deity is a deep, intrinsic felt-experience, not a superior being or companion.

A god outside nature would be a busy god indeed. Creation is not over with the big bang. A god that created the universe must recreate it every moment

The shift to one from many gods with sequestration of feeling is like a turn from promiscuity to fixation on the beloved

To extract spirit from nature is to extract mind as well. The perception of nature and the nature of perception depend on mind. A mind-independent nature is unknowable.

Traces of the religious can be found in the worship of the beloved

If you are not religious, at least have reverence for the mystery.

Advocates of causal change take god to be superfluous

For a gene with 20% penetrance, the 80% left to chance—the complexity of experience—is interpreted as fate or god's will.

God survives in the disparity of fact with evidence. Every discovery is another field for exploration.

The more we know, the more we realize how little we know. Could we say, science serves deity by increasing the limits of the unknowable?

Examine the god of the philosophers, not that of religious institutions. Argue with Plotinus or Augustine, not straw men and fairy tales.

Whitehead's process god as companion is a god of becoming in nature, closer to the spirit of passage than an almighty being.

To those who fear an eternal afterlife, there is comfort in an impersonal deity.

The thought of god inspires to greatness. The thought of death gives urgency to inspiration.

The perfection of god in the imagination is an ideal for the subjective aim.

The belief in god rests above and below in the passage of categories.

The absolute as origination, the noosphere as destination; an arising as creation, a perishing as destruction, with meaning in the transition of wholes to parts. The pattern of transition in the mental state engenders belief in a transcendent being (category).

Spirit

To experience the spiritual, do not cross the bridge, dive in the river.

THE SPIRITUAL IS THE sense of mind external, or the extension of inner mind into or as the world. In the primitive, the dream world continues into the animated world of consciousness surrounding a thin veil of practical reason. The mysterious events of dream and it's affinity with myth belong to an outer realm of spirit, a world of meaningfulness without meaning, in which man, a creaturely presence, in nakedness and vulnerability, is as much imagination as real. Generally, spirituality implies god or a sense of the divine, but reverence for an animating power in nature does not entail that it emanate from or is the body of god, though an insubstantial and incomplete process aligned with and part of the natural process can be a source of comfort if not companionship. A world of spirit has its origins in the mind, but since animistic feeling is not apprehended as a projection of the observer, it most often has its explanation in god as source and culmination. To experience the Divine is to be one with nature as an emanation of god.

The spiritual may arise as an intuition that nature is apprehended in the imagination as a psychic, not physical, reality. If there is no direct knowledge of the real, and if all nature is phenomenal, mentality is pervasive, and spirituality is closer to the mental then the material world. If the relation of mind to brain is analogous to that of god to nature, the expansion of psyche to god or the concentration of divinity in an individual mind, create a continuum of mentality and spirit parallel with that of brain and physical nature. Whether a mind is a condensation of spirit, or spirit is an expansion of mind, the continuum provides an explanatory basis for the belief in the actuality of the divine as a realm of spirit.

We have no immediate experience of the brain activity that generates the mind; experience is of brain as a mental object, a model, a specimen or object for research. We are not inclined to believe we create a brain out of psyche or that nature is created out of the mind of god, but it is less implausible that if brain can elaborate a mind, nature might elaborate mentality.

The proto-psychic is not the compliment or gift of mind to the physical, but the source of the mentality into which the physical evolves.

Could we say evolutionary growth increases spirituality? If human mind contributes to the idea of god, does it also add to the presence of divinity, or to the spirituality that supports this intuition?

༄

God is to thought as a soul is to the self

The energy in a particle becomes the feeling in a mind

If god is the sum of mind in the universe, does each individual mind contribute to god?

Are we spirit in god›s mind, or is god the collective spirit of all minds?

My writing may not convince others but it may convince me

If god does not exist, what is there to doubt? If doubt is a proof of existence or consciousness, why is it not so for god?

The question is not what difference would it make if god does not exist, but what would exist if there is no god to make a difference.

I think reverence is an acceptable substitute for faith.

Simplicity in mind is obscured by the complexity necessary to perceive it

The words that convey thoughts fracture the beliefs that underlie them

Adding up statements reinforces an argument but does not constitute a proof

Immediacy of contact is the cost of the aboutness of the intentional

Before you believe in god, the belief must already be there.

Mysticism

The existence of the mystical may not be rational but it is feeling, not reason, on which existence depends.

THE MYSTICAL IS NOT rooted out by scientific progress but propagates in what science leaves unexplained. There is reverence for mystery, not an expectation that a full accounting of mind and nature awaits scientific discovery; there is potentiality in all entities, not certainty of structure; there is covert process in substance; and there is sensitivity to a deeper order in the transition from energy to feeling and from becoming to being. The theory preserves the uniformity of the mystical spirit without the trappings of hastily-formed beliefs. Primarily, it applies to the spiritual, even to a quality of divinity that is known by intuition and exists outside the sphere of reason (which for the mystical frame of mind is a parched desert compared to the life-giving soul of nature).

Mysticism takes many forms—the poet, the yoga, the priest, the philosopher—but the belief in spirit, the incompleteness of materialism, and the mystery of creation are common to all. So too is the urge for an occasion of immediacy of spiritual experience, of mind-external, as Wordsworth wrote of sense as "the anchor of my purest thoughts". The mystic is often a panpsychic, as am I, a living presence in the lowliest of entities, unwilling to concede a Rubicon in evolution for the appearance of consciousness and value. It is one thing to reduce mind to brain, or to gene, or to physics, and quite another to go in the reverse direction, from superstrings and microphysics to human thought. I would say the pre-condition for mentality is not proto-psyche or proto-consciousness but energy in the inanimate, which becomes feeling in organic nature. This passes to instinctual drive and its objects, then to conceptual-feeling and consciousness with its essential quality of intentional desire.

Reflections on Mind and the Image of Reality

For one who thinks in a creative way, there is also the magic in the creative process, inspiration and the feeling of novelty out of nothingness, which gives a sense of a power beyond logic and the force of unconscious ideas streaming into consciousness. If we are open and receptive, we feel a sense of the unknown that surrounds us from the deep well of unconscious thought; the traits of past existences, an inheritance of which we are dimly aware; the continuity with forgotten strains of ancestral becoming before humans walked the plains; patterns that bind us to earth and animal feeling, and to the foundational process from which life arose, all of which, intuited within the most ordinary act, can be recovered in a gradual and prepared descent to the shadows.

༄

Is it metaphysics or mysticism to suppose that process is uniform though its manifestations are diverse?

Help me to listen to the blades of grass that cry out as they are trampled underfoot. Help me to give thanks for a life sustained by creaturely sacrifice. And help me to feel my own death as a replenishment of the sustenance nature has provided.

༄

The wind that awakens the stillness of the leaves is a harbinger of the sleep to follow.

That which is before me obscures my vision for that which I want to see.

Spirit may be invisible to sight and inaudible to sound but attentive, it is palpable in feeling.

To avoid distraction is one thing, but an empty mind is a vacancy.

Sacrifice of realness is the crucial step from focal concentration to unhindered meditation.

The less real, the more meaningful; absolute reality does not reveal its meaningfulness.

To lapse into a category is still not to abandon concepts. Without concepts there is sheer multiplicity, not emptiness.

Atheism

*The atheist does not have to defend his point of view,
merely exploit the vulnerabilities of theism*

I CAN BELIEVE THAT unicorns do not exist but am open to the possibility they have existed, will exist, or can be found elsewhere in the universe. At any rate, my conviction is not strong though I am certain it is true, but this is of little consequence in my life. To believe that something does not exist is a belief in what, exactly? To believe that god does not exist, whether a personal god of miracles or a sense of divinity in nature, is to believe in nothing with no evidence one way or another in the matter. A strong belief in something that does not exist, as in an assertive atheism, exhibits a strong conviction for a belief in nothing. This demonstrates that the content of the belief—true, false or nebulous—is less important in conviction than the emotional investment to believe in no matter what that something is.

Still, it is puzzling that some—mostly minor—philosophers get so heated about the non-existence of an entity, spirit, power, which is no less an act of faith than that which they criticize. In that a forceful atheism merely dismisses arguments for the existence of god or divinity in nature *tout court*, it resembles a philosophy of eliminativism, in which mentality ceases to be problematic when it is denied or reduced to brain. Rational arguments for the existence or non-existence of the divine are irrelevant to faith or conviction, no more than reason explains an interest in history or entomology, or the objects of love, disdain or envy, or why go on living or fighting illness when we all die anyway, or the beauty of art, poetry or music, or the joys and pains of family. Most of what makes life livable has nothing to do with reason, so that to apply reason to faith, or to deny spirit on lack of evidence, is no different from denying all the pleasure and meaning of life because they cannot be rationally justified.

Further, arguments against religion that critique miracles, holy wars, church doctrine, the belief in a personal god that intervenes, reincarnation, heaven or an after-life, are irrelevant to the presence of a divine power, a god of process within nature and part of it—nature outside and inside. Such arguments attack the accoutrements of institutional doctrine, crimes in the name of religion, or the absence of evidence for a personal god, claiming inconsistency with the invariant laws of physics and the belief in a mindless and purely mechanical universe, which is not an irrefutable truth but also an act of faith or conviction in science.

In India, there has been little unrest of a large underclass, which could potentially be provoked to an uprising. Conflict of one class or religion against another, poor and rich, suppressed and privileged, tends to be orchestrated by a cynical, ambitious and/or revolutionary elite. In Sofia in 1976, I was told that the problem was not communism; it was communism for the people and capitalism for the communists. The few exploit the many, and enforce or inspire aggression or submission. The subject/object divide is a false narrative of alienation, not the basis for unrest, discord or perpetual revolution. In any event, to know that the world and its objects are penetrated through and through by subjectivity, that of the observer and that intrinsic to the object, and to know that the self is not independent of its objects, provides a modicum of understanding and a basis for a community of shared values.

༺

Overall, I believe the teachings of religion, were they to be followed, are a force for good in the world.

Conflicts or missteps attributed to religion pale in comparison to those of atheist societies, such as Nazis and Communists.

The Crusades, you say, were slaughters in the name of religion, but estimates are that no more than 2000 were killed. Yet what do religious atrocities have to do with the existence of god?

Atheists are fond of quoting Einstein but not his close friend and colleague at Princeton, the great mathematician, Gödel, who was a devout believer, nor do they mention the best philosophers of the last century, James, Bradley and Whitehead.

Is the agnostic hedging his bets, waiting for evidence or just weak in the knees?

Atheism

Religion no more restrains brutality than encourages it. Apart from *ex cathedra* mandates like the Decalogue, which can be reduced to the Golden Rule, belief in god does not directly impact moral law.

The concept of god as an impersonal force in nature, though not consoling, allows mute worship at the silent throne of deity.

The conviction that god does not exist makes a fetish of absence.

The gradient from dream to object has an illusion that feels real at one end and an image of the real at the other.

Ironic that the light of consciousness, the outcome of evolution, sees only blind process in its origins.

Belligerence, ambition and lust for power are the instinctual drivers of conflict, with religion its justification.

The morality from instruction in values in childhood is stronger than that of the church.

Does conviction in atheism drive the debate or does competitiveness attempt to silence opposition?

Like an animal that senses weakness in a prey, the atheist goes in for the kill.

Refutation is time lost, lacks invention and won't help you plead your case at the gates of heaven.

A mystical intuition of god, like all phenomena, is illusory, but still is a powerful experience to which the atheist is refractory.

The greatest of the artists, thinkers and scientists held a vision of deity as representing order, harmony and perfection as the goal of their work. Deity was not a source but a model for the subjective aim.

Don't you think something vital is lost when spirit is routed from nature?

Religious beliefs are constantly replaced by science. A spiritual life is regnant in the incompleteness of scientific explanation that leaves a residue of the insoluble.

Perhaps spirit lies in the unknown but without it we might be unaware of the limits of scientific explanation.

Hard to believe that in dying we enter the reality that eluded us in life.

Optimism

*The silver lining in every cloud is a streak of
lightning that signals a downpour*

THE OPTIMIST IS NECESSARILY a short-term thinker since the longer the wait, the more likely—indeed, it is inevitable—that things will turn out badly. Pessimism is more rational, certainly over the long term, for it is aligned with the cycles of life and the certainty of terminal despair. The optimist is hopeful, positive, which alone can improve immediate outcomes. Both are self-fulfilling. A hopeful outlook may improve physical well-being, the reverse for a negative one. The optimist may be proved wrong but the pessimist is ultimately right. Optimism becomes euphoria when it leaves its grounding in the real; pessimism becomes morbid ideation with a loss of interest in life. There is a contagion in the positivity of a forward-looking attitude, infecting others with the delusion of happy endings, a marriage that will last forever, children who will always love their parents, the upward mobility of individual and class that provides modest relief from the bitterness and despondency that afflicts so many on the planet, including the philosophically-minded who interpret experience from a strictly objective standpoint.

    The psychologist who takes a resolutely externalist perspective, denying subjectivity or reducing it to the brain—were his argument consistent with his life—would necessarily be the dourest of companions, given a radical elimination of mind and the inner life. This way of thinking turns feeling, goals and beliefs into neural firings, relegating hopefulness or optimism to delusional thinking or, at best, a biological marker for extinction by way of innocence, or survival through positivity and failure to succumb to hopelessness. Of course, the arguments of the externalist are also a machine output that has little to recommend it beyond the logical possibilities available to the software which they, or others, have engineered. There is something jarring about seeing an externalist enjoying an outing with his children—little computing machines—or enjoying the acoustic noise and auditory pattern recognition that incites the pleasure centers listening to Bach. In the elimination of the subjective, including a self, the resolute materialist should care as little for himself or others as for his car or computer, that is, if he believes with every sinew of his being that his philosophy is true for otherwise he is a sham.

In contrast, the optimist, though no doubt aware of real and potential danger, takes a position in opposition to externalism, or at least he carries on as if the subjective is real, that feelings, desires and aspirations matter and are as real, if not more so, than sheer physicality. Optimism is an act of faith, founded on the implicit belief that life will be good or better in the future, that an illness can be cured, that problems will pass and that one's expectations and better nature will come through. It is, I think, an inborn tendency to promote striving for betterment, overcoming of obstacles and pain, and a protection against debilitation, fatalism, emptiness and the encircling void. The fleetingness of pleasure does not contract the search for it, indeed, the urge that the externalist attributes to brain activity or an outcome of self-preservative drive, may well be the basis for the common belief, at least to middle age that things will improve.

Moreover, optimism encourages agency while pessimism leads to passivity and defeat. The optimist does not believe things will improve without effort, so there is a disincentive to give up and accept whatever comes to pass. The pessimist, who expects the worst, has little reason to try to make it better. This attitude need not lead to despair. Masses of people who live in poverty may accept their condition and find pleasure where they can. We enter and depart this world as unwilling victims, but in youth, the departure is far off in an unimaginable future, the life-urge is so powerful, the flicker of passing time so imperceptible, the despair of others and their condemnation to a life of sickness and hunger largely invisible, that the struggles of so many have, for most, little to do with the confidence in one's self and one's future.

A friend of mine, a noted psychologist, once asked a hundred or so patients in a hospital as to their happiness and hopefulness regardless of the gravity or extent of disability. The striking finding was that most of them were hopeful of a good outcome of health and survival. One might call this denial, but is that not just a psychiatric label for innate optimism? However, like repression or sublimation, denial implies a psychic mechanism when a positive attitude mitigates a disheartening certainty. The outcome of mistaken optimism is acceptance and resignation, not pessimism.

Damage to both frontal lobes gives a person who does not dwell on the future and has a cheerful attitude to events—even to the point of joking—an indifference to emotional pain or deprivation. This also occurs in frontal lobotomy. Tertiary syphilis gives megalomania as an unrealistic and grandiose expectation, sincerely held, of future accomplishment. This is more than optimism; it has a delusional quality.

Nietzsche is an example of someone whom syphilitic megalomania became delusion. The optimism in the face of incurable cancer or someone judged as brain-dead, could be said to border on the irrational and in this sense approximates delusion. Such cases might imply that optimism is a pathological state, but it is more accurate to say pathology unveils a fundamental attitude of positivity that is mitigated by a trust in objective knowledge. For the pessimistic philosopher, and there are many, optimism is a state of innocence, *naïveté* or self-deception. For one who prizes the unvarnished truth, the evanescence, fragility and illusoriness of life, the misery of so many, the selfishness, egoism and dispassion of humankind, can lead to no other attitude. For the optimist, especially one who is pacific in the face of death and has an anthropocentric view of the universe, or a firm belief in deity, pessimism is a self-defeating and imprudent philosophy that offers little more than complaints about the human condition.

Max Picard wrote a 300 page tome on silence. Artists who believe life is a "cosmic joke" still sign their works. Philosophers who write of the vanity and meaninglessness of existence have their names on their book jackets.

A simple act of kindness is worth more than a treatise on emptiness.

The irony in pessimism is the disconnect between what you say or write and how you live.

Hölderlin thought that great art must always be mindful of death. Munch appears to have been haunted by this thought. Fear of death can be a vaccine against suicide.

Yet suicide is more common in peace than war; more in the well-off than the poor. Epicurean suicide (Durkheim) occurs in a mood of ironic tranquility.

Are optimism and pessimism the natural outcomes of feeling and reason? Feeling drives us forward; reason stops us in our tracks.

Optimism

One might speak of fate in a genetic disease that is bound to appear at some point in life, but not if the gene can be removed or blocked. Here, as with all instances, present ignorance conditions future outcomes

The tragic is a kind of doom awaiting the unsuspecting.

We revel in the downfall of a great man, since their high position nulls compassion and we envy their success, while the ordinary have less to lose and, regardless of status, most are destined for unhappiness.

Tragedy is a fall from high position. Pessimism is tragedy as a universal.

A worthy enemy can be more useful than a host of friends.

An opinion of someone forms rapidly and no amount of effort can change it.

A tactless remark to a person of influence can unwittingly derail a career.

The optimist magnifies the happiness that is derided by the pessimist.

Pessimism may replace optimism but optimism can overcome it.

The fact that we are fated to die is the psychological root of tragedy. The fall from greatness is a death in life.

Can one speak of an intrinsic and inescapable fate of the body that establishes the lifespan, health, intelligence, and an extrinsic fate to which the person is a party to change in the world?

If we could manipulate the genes to prevent aging and multiply intelligence and other faculties, could we say that fate is contingent?

The incongruous in comedy is the inevitable in tragedy. The ironic is pessimism intruding on the incongruence of optimism.

With exceptions, comedy and optimism are for the present; tragedy and pessimism for the future. One brings light to darkness, the other the reverse.

Optimism is perhaps founded on pessimism for it is open to doubt. I can say I am hopeful of living another five years but think it unlikely, or I wish to live even if the years will not be worth living.

PART III

The Political Animal

How do we maintain our individuality
while remaining part of society?

Conflict

*The battle between ideas tends to be fought in the world,
not in the mind where it belongs*

SUBJECTIVITY RESULTS IN THE objectification of the person and the world. Even in objectification, in conformance, opposition or abeyance, the person is an occasion of self, in which habit collides with an insistent potential for renewal. To treat a person as an object is to malign, to marginalize or exploit. It is also a denial of value; the individuality of the person is worthless. Conversely, to say a person or thing has value (quality of internal feeling), or to say what the person is worth (quantity of external value), is a perspective, as in praising the beauty of a diamond or discussing its cost. A person or any object can be observed aesthetically (subjective process) or as a product (final actuality). The subjective judgment has one foot in the world, while the objective judgment is fully external. Each mode of valuation has a common origin, one a category in which the object is an end, the other in which the object is a means, but the categories are successive (earlier and later) segments in the mind/brain state.

The other can be monstrous, but monsters, tyrants, leaders, celebrities, holy men, arise out of personal disposition and the needs of followers. They do not fall out of the sky but embody a conscious or unconscious tradition and the will of acolytes. Individual bias intensifies the support of like-minded groups. Dostoevsky wrote that we all have within us a child murderer. Victor Hugo wrote, *"nous sommes deux au fond de notre esprit"*, by which he meant good and evil in every heart. We have leaders and adversaries who we are primed to fight or follow, but the embedded relation with others generally shares attributes of a group. Self and other, Hegel wrote, arise in a single act but others are multiples and the self is specified out of a manifold. The other appears in the act of self-creation. It is well to keep in mind that objects and others have two faces, one the mental image we create and one that is authentically theirs, i.e. subjective quality and material reality.

Subjectivism does not imply relativism. Dewey said facts are irreducible values. The fact is not independent of the feeling that makes it relevant. This does not mean absolute truth is unknowable or that different truths are equivalent. It implies that consensus and social forces, whatever they may be, enter into the adaptive world of thought. Adaptive process in humans can facilitate or vitiate uniformity, but across cultures and environments it allows for distinctions in thought, language and action. The Darwinian struggle is less an internal adaptive process than its extra-psychic consequences, that is, it is a population effect, not a process in the individual organism. Still, the outcome of the clash of need with reality is a person in conflict or in harmony with an objectified world.

Psychoanalysis makes a similar error, importing external events into the mind as causal agencies. The unconscious conflict that is essential to psychoanalytic theory and treatment entails thematic recurrence applied to changing situations. This conflict is inferred from behavior and dream. Commonly, a kernel of (early) life experience persists like an atavistic trait to influence behaviors decades later. In contrast, conscious conflict—a "to be or not to be"—is a failure of one option to individuate with sufficient clarity or to prevail by an emotional tug. The mulling of options tends to engage the same or similar (object or temporal) categories, e.g. what dress to buy, what film to see, what job to take, not a clash of beliefs or a choice of film and future vacation. Conscious choice, as Hume argued, is largely emotive, while the unconscious sequence navigates possibilities that, except for the survivors, remain unborn or virtual.

∾

The psychoanalysts internalize conflict, e.g. a child and its parents, as an unconscious struggle within a psychic domain when conflict is an extrinsic relation of self to others, ideas, substances, logical solids.

Indecision is not necessarily conflict; rather uncertainty, hesitation or weakness of will. Ultimately, process is attenuated at a categorical phase before act or object emerges.

In the conflict of individual and society, the morality of the inner is either/or, that of the outer, better/worse.

CONFLICT

You know I get annoyed
Whenever you are citing Freud
Often false but never new
The theory ages less than you
Just keep talking to expose
On the couch in still repose
Seeds of trauma bearing fruit
Apply the same for each recruit

Adaptation

*To adapt is to exploit and prosper. Intelligence is a tool
that pries adaptation from immediate contact.*

A STRIVING FOR FITNESS that entails competition among organisms is equivalent to the elicitation of objects in the mind. Organisms and objects adapt; those that best adapt recur, momentarily in survival and replication, secondarily in offspring, and continuously in the mental state. A mental state, an object, an organism, is realized for an instant as a final actuality. The recurrence of minds and individuals realizes an aim to definiteness. The arising and perishing of the mental state is a microcosm of the birth and death of organisms, of societies, of universes.

A central feature of adaptation is that organisms exist as a negative image of the real. To achieve fitness in an environment is to be sculpted by what is lacking, necessary or available. Surviving elimination is the counterpoint of sensibility. That which is, is molded by that which is not, as the left hand needs the right hand to clasp them together. An organism fulfills a role, unscripted, by trial and error. A sessile plant in the ocean is a contrast to that which shapes its existence. It is predator and prey for other organisms that are as much a part of the Umwelt as the physical environment. Every organism must survive a hostile environment, and satisfy a need that is the reciprocal to that of the niche in which it exists. The shaping of that which evolves gives a mirror image of what exists, as a crack in a rock shapes the weed that breaks through.

Adaptation raises the problem of the reality to which an organism adapts. The organism arises in and elaborates a functional space created by the environment. Survival is recurrent existence that requires continuous adaptation. The strength and agility of one organism is the weakness or maladroitness of another. The grass that feeds an animal strives to return

Adaptation

the next season. Reciprocity, like gender, is the driving force of selection. The human mind apprehends this drama as an aim to fitness through competing pressures, while the mind itself, as an evolved entity constrained by sensation, in the same way the organism is shaped by the environment, is a complementarity to the reality to which it adapts. Reality seems to be on the other side of this mirror, as in a Cocteau film or Escher drawing, like matter to antimatter, resembling that which it duplicates.

∽

The physical organism adapts, but the mind also evolves to enhance adaptation. Physical adaptation is comprehensible but the nature of mind, which seems free of necessity, is also an adaptive organism for which we pay for in philosophical confusion.

Trillions of microorganisms yet to be described form a living foundation from which the visible evolves.

Survival in an organism becomes success in human mind, with intelligence the means to achieve it.

One view of intelligence is that of resolving, avoiding or profiting from risky situations.

The ability to solve problems entails departure from routine. This liberates the organism from habitual response. Novel acts are elicited in a category or by overlap with other categories.

Unlike reason, intelligence includes an affective component. Sometimes the most intelligent course is to suspend reason and follow common sense.

> Years of study, writing books,
> Within a scholar's moldy nooks
> Some are led to concentrate
> Avoiding subjects that relate
> Assured their focus will prevail
> On topics that the works entail
> While others deeper to the source
> Of process and instinctual force
> Build upon a slender reed
> A tree of knowledge from a seed

Freedom

Thought is limitless; action is constrained.

How do we explain freedom when all roads lead to determinism, when conscious choice is a product of unconscious disposition, of biases, loyalties and habits, and if options are the illusory alternatives to actions predetermined by core beliefs and feeling? Even in the volitional lifting of a finger, sub-surface oscillations accompany unconscious activation.

What would it take for a choice to be free? Probably one that was novel, creative or opposed to bias, indifferent to personal advantage, out of character and one that reflects rational judgment even if contrary to the interests of the agent. Yet in a choice, say for the better good even at personal expense, the decision can still be seen as a boon to the agent, an enhancement of status, a desire to be worthy and praised. If choices are limited and decisions ordained, am I still not free to think of any act or idea no matter how terrible, subversive, criminal or implausible? My thoughts can range over any topic, fantastic or imaginary, and consider choices that will never be implemented.

Every act arises out of a penumbra of other possibilities. The alternative to an action is inaction or another action. The possibility of another action makes me question the action that occurs. This does not mean my action is incorrect, but that it may betray other acts that are better. Choices are driven by character. Except for bad luck, in choice there are no "what might have beens". Perhaps the choice was unwise or a better choice was not noticed, or the choice was correct but there was an unexpected change in events. As in the song, *je ne regrette rien,* my lack of regret is a fact I regret. Is it a sign of complaisance, self-satisfaction or resignation? If I acted within my limits, how can I regret an inability to act otherwise? One cannot forecast illness or a brick falling on your head, but one can regret a poor decision, a failure to act or a misjudgment. Unless choices are fully determined in a world of hard causation, there is always a "what if" in every act: what if I left my apartment five minutes earlier, accepted an invitation, challenged a speaker, and so on. My decisions were instinctive. When I had to weigh options I sensed unease. Should one choose who to marry? Socrates, asked whether a young man should marry, was said to reply, whatever you do you'll regret it.

The illusion of freedom does not come from the inescapability of causation but the unconscious origin of conscious acts. Nothing that we do happens for the reasons we think. A reason explains or justifies. It is a response to asking, what is the point? The point is in asking the question, not in justifying the outcome, since that is unknown when the decision is made. Asking expands the horizon of thought for another round of action. For this reason, every act is a gesture of faith.

Of course, action carries consequences but consequences, harmful or punitive, are extrinsic regulators of action, and do not impact directly the idea of free will. If we lived in a lawless, narcissistic, hedonistic society in which rape, murder, pillage and so on were not punished—though there would be resistance and opposing force—would the will not then be free to act as it may? Values limit choices, but the real check on action is not conscience or basic goodness but a system of laws that delimit options, the shoulds and should not's of behavior, inculcated early in life.

Basically, there are two constraints on freedom: (1) punishment that engenders restraint; and (2) values that regulate acts. Such are the Scylla of belief and the Charybdis of condemnation through which we navigate. If the thought of an act is free even if the act is not, what is the relation of thought or action to freedom?

There are several ways to interpret this observation. It may be that we do not act on imagination but exclude unrealistic ideas or that options arise independent of conceptual possibilities. It may be that such possibilities narrow down to two or three adaptive solutions or that outcomes and consequences implicit in desire cancel unrealistic goals. I may want something I can't afford, or desire someone knowing I will be rejected. We internalize these external impediments as obstacles to action that would otherwise be free. Actions that are inconsistent with character are infrequent, often requiring drugs, alcohol, altered states or the support of a gang or crowd to mitigate responsibility. We say the person loses inhibitions, or has weakness of character, but it entails a lowering of adaptive constraints.

The regulation of behavior concerns not only immediate acts but also the projection of extra-sensory desires into the future (such as a bank robbery that engages not only values but the anticipation of outcomes). These may not dissuade an individual from planning the robbery or other acts, like suicide (a sudden impulse to a foolish action—the prevention of which requires intrinsic self-control to underlie or run parallel to action-development). This is as much a part of freedom or its lack as action. If we all have a child murderer within us, it is safely buried or suppressed to a degree that it is rarely a viable option. Is this because it is outweighed by values or societal constraints or that the momentary state and conditions are not conducive to such an action?

Generally, the more outlandish, anti-social or fantastic thoughts tend to occur when a suspension of ordinary behavior and decision-making becomes the dominant focus of possibility. Even then the decision comes down to whether or not to act. If imaginative acts arise when action is curtailed, it is unlikely that action will be triggered by that which occurs in its delay. Further, it is not only the wish, or the multitude of potential acts that drives the sense of freedom, nor the ability to imagine whatever one wants, or even the capacity to produce change in the imagination—such as imaging a mouse running on the back of an elephant—but the decision among competing choices, which is the most constrained and least free of all actions. Specifically, it is the transition of thought to action that limits freedom, or free will, not the capacity to imagine most any action.

Thus, free will comes down to choice prior to action, as wide-ranging possibilities in thought contract to options to be exercised. The options are conditioned by intrinsic values and extrinsic impediments. We can say that intrinsic factors—values, beliefs, biases, habits and so on—determine choices, but these are no more defining than social norms, punishment, accusation and the like. Thought is clearly free until action is in play, unless the choice of an action depends largely on external conditions.

Could we still maintain that will is not free if an action could change circumstance? There is irony in the fact that thought is free until it narrows down to decision, and then, presumably, to action, which generally entails a yes/no to a sequence of implementations. If thought is free but restrained in action, which in turn is limited *inter alia* by character and consequence, can we say that freedom of thought, and free will, are real but conditioned by ancillary and largely extrinsic factors?

Looking back over my life and seeing it *en bloc*, it seems that it unfolded according to a plan. Certainly it was not my plan. Like others, I was ignorant of the different paths to be taken, what should have been decided and the outcome. Yet still it seems that much of what happened, barring bad luck, could not have been otherwise.

∽

Will began as an impulse in drive, whittled down to a vague hope or wishful idea, finally in disillusion evaporated in a trickle of lapsed intent.

The thoughtful person would like a life of action, but the latter does not fancy a life of thought. Bertrand Russell and Joseph Conrad are examples.

We want the whole self to go into action but too often the self stays behind as an observer.

The inability to decide results in inaction, but that is not its intended outcome.

Hesitation is the seed of voluntariness.

The failure to decide is not necessarily a sign of thought. It can be weakness of will (akrasia).

The passive individual may have an active imagination but avoids choice. Is the transfer of decision to others an act of will or its failure?

When we contrast decisiveness with passivity, we see the effect of agency on choice. Does this concern free will, or is it merely a sign of an inward or outgoing personality?

Too many options leads to uncertainty, not freedom.

Even when one's fate is sealed—old age, execution, suicide—there is the freedom to whine or be courageous.

One can say, courage in the face of death is the ultimate act of freedom, especially if it is willed (Hume).

Having a life plan and sticking to it latches freedom to a goal.

If choices are not freely decided, what is the point of deliberation? Perhaps it is the inevitable result of intentional consciousness. But what is the point of that?

In a "locked-in" syndrome with a brainstem stroke, a person is totally paralyzed except for eye movements. Thought, even complex ideation, is spared. There is absolute freedom of thought with near-impossibility of action. Such freedom, like the thoughts of one buried alive, at least when sudden, is terrifying. Yet, Stephen Hawking astonishes the world.

The illusion of freedom does not come from the inescapability of causation but the unconscious origin of conscious acts.

Freedom from the noumenal includes the brain as well as sensibility. There is also habit and disposition.

Does this mean the only freedom is thought before commitment?

The freedom to act does not mean the action is free

Action forecloses possibilities that are essential to choice

The sense of freedom clings to a slender thread between habit and perception

We interpret choice as freedom unaware of options undisclosed

Things are real when illusions cohere, but they are recognized as illusory compared to deeper layers of illusion

Sanity may perceive illusion but does not feel it. The danger is not in belief but in feeling

Conviction is strong in false belief; unshakeable in delusion. Certainty without conviction is tentative.

Truth plays no role in conviction.

Why regret an unfortunate decision if a correct one plays out in a parallel universe?

Would you be happy with a perfect clone left by your lover?

Remorse is for hurt to others, regret for the self

One can regret a lost benefit from a friend who missed an opportunity

Introspection has its dangers; too close and you may fall in

Profound insight totters on the edge of an abyss

The valuation in a fact points to the subjectivity that keeps it alive

The price of wisdom is often the temptation of madness

The creative delves into the unknown where beauty and monsters are waiting.

The possibilities of the known are a fraction of the concealed

Truth as the elimination of error is one error away from refutation

A thing is pruned to specificity. Yes, one is conscious of the final negation but a veto goes all the way down

Put differently, the veto at the final phase repeats the pruning below.

I had a dream that underwent multiple revisions before awakening, each a more hopeful version of the last. This implies unconscious shaping of the final outcome

For a single word, thought engages all of mind. There are no bits of information or memory stores. The trace of a word is the track of its actualization.

In each selection what is discarded is the cost of what is retained

The basic law of process is the sculpting of irrelevance, a passage from generality to precision like the *via negativa* in the description of god

The final word or object is not selected; it is what remains

Freedom

In the garden, a cutting of branches brings new flowers to bloom
Discovery is uncovering the potential hidden in what is already known

> A mental state grows and dies
> Others in its place arise
> Segments in the state survive
> Some to perish, some to thrive

Independent, you say, but you host a trillion microorganisms that will feast on your remains

Leisure is the luxury of aging if you know what to do with it

Stress is not only indecision and internal tension. There is an effect on the body/world divide. Even in a psychic world, the impact of sensibility is abrupt.

Wrapped like insulation on a looping sewage drain, the world around the body flows through it end to end

If fate determines good and bad luck, for every moment of every entity and every piece of matter in the universe, complexity is just a compounding of causal laws.

The fluid, open future is frozen in the fixed, changeless past; the one, possibility, the other, inevitability.

> Is it luck, is it fate
> That causal laws anticipate
> Or any instant can detect
> The not-yet future we expect
> Change seems centered in the flow
> Of causal pairs we think we know
> But not the phases in-between
> Alleged by all but never seen

The problem for mental causation is that actions explained by reason, or delusion, are propelled by feeling, which is not rationally analyzable. If I lift my finger or cross my legs, the only explanation I can give is, I felt like it. The question is how far down the evolutionary scale does this go?

Value

Value has one foot in the mind, the other in the world.

THE EMOTIONAL QUALITY OF concepts spills out into the feeling that accompanies them. Love grows in the concept of the beloved, not in the object. As the concept specifies an object, feeling remains internal, except for what is centered as value in the object. Love is a growth of the affective tonality of the conceptual phase in object-formation, not internalization but a coming-to-the-fore of buried segments. Except for value, emotions remain largely in the imagination. A diamond has personal and economic value. She (a diamond, a pet) is wonderful (desirable, unique, etc.) because I love her (it), or I love her because she is wonderful. The enhanced value of the beloved, like that of other precious objects, is not love but a psychic manifestation of need and/or desire. One can say, I love my ring, my home, my car, which points to its valuation. This is related to but unlike love for another, which is an internal state bound up with category-formation and idealization.

∽

    Love is the ultimate in positive valuation, hate in negative, but fear and hunger import value to other objects
        Desire implements a portion of the value that comes from drive
        The sum of your values, not your acts, is who you are
        Belief is the framework within which value arises.
        Or one can say, values form the seeds from which beliefs will grow
        The relation of belief to value is that of concept to feeling
        Beliefs lead to concepts that deposit objects. Values are ascribed to wants and desires that accompany concepts into objects
        Belief is the conceptual portion of a forming object or idea, value its affective quality. Every feeling realizes a belief, every concept has a value
        The transition to actuality of conceptual-feeling is a becoming-into-being

Value

From inner to outer and back, acquaintance returns to imagination as prelude to love or friendship.

In the mind, value is a mode of loving; in the world, a mode of worth

Economic theory applies to the inanimate, but the mental process in love is the same

The source of value is the trickle of affect that flows out with the object

To see the other objectively is to extinguish value, endorse judgment and relinquish the ideal

An entity in the world has no intrinsic value, only material existence; an object in the world has value and meaning

Not only love, but existence is reinstated in every surge of feeling

Purpose in life as fulfillment of design must be prior to our striving

> What is a meaningful life in a world without meaning?
> What is purpose in a world of blind chance?
> I ask because what evolves in man is not evident in nature

In animals, the instinctual drive that targets objects shrinks in man to desire.

Value in animals goes directly to the object, in shelter, predation or mating.

Animal purposefulness becomes human agency when ideas replace objects

The emergence of higher states—agency, meaning, value, language, belief—is less likely than a continuum all the way down

∽

First, feeling generates existence, then interest, then value, as it narrows the field to a focus on one object. Interest partitions a multitude of possibilities to a concrete other, as what begins with a focus of attention becomes a center of value. The field narrows down to the object of interest as phases in perception grow in the mind. In a state of intense love (or fear), other objects fade into the background and all one sees is the beloved (danger).

The category of mother includes innumerable others, but the category of Sylvia, my mother, includes only one. Value confines the attributes of the member to a limited set. These are uniformly positive in love, with the complementary process in hate. God as love, Satan as evil, represent this process in its other-worldly manifestation. They are the only members of unique and opposing categories, idealized in the attribution of qualities to a sole instance. In this way, a parent becomes an ideal, a paragon of motherhood, of love and devotion, or perhaps of meanness and indifference, against which other individuals are compared.

∾

The basis of love and creation retraces the path from self to world

Thought is deviation in memory; memory is replication in thought

Love at first sight reminds us that love, as with all feeling, is wholly endogenous

A small crack in an egg and the contents seep out

So too love with a tear in the heart

Seek a counselor and what love you had is lost. But a withering of love is often what it takes to save a token bond

Lovers betrayed who turn sorrow to anger destroy what their own imagination has created

Jealousy is less the fear of loss than injury to the self

When true love is over, do not blame the other. The sources of joy and grief rest in the imagination

> So it seemed you came to me
> As love developed naturally
> Two in one as a connection
> One in two as pure invention
> Love does not by linkage come
> Unity is not a sum
> An image I alone selected
> You, my soul, resurrected

Every mental act begins with drive (hunger, sexual), which specifies unconscious need to conscious desire. In genuine love, they are aligned. The demands of the unconscious are mirrored in conscious wish. In the passage from drive to desire, the unconscious core develops to a self as the origin of a conscious aim. The self gives an act, an image or object, as an outcome, or as the content of an intentional consciousness. This idea is beautifully rendered in the film, *Belle du Jour*, where conscious reason is trumped by unconscious need. The unfortunate husband might have said he tried to love his wife but that kindness was no substitute for unconscious need in one driven or accustomed to abuse.

When the beloved is lost, intentional feeling should have nowhere to go, but the idea of the beloved was always its target

Adapting to Society

While success depends on individuality, survival (or adaptive success) depends on the immersion of individuality in a group

DIFFERENT INDIVIDUALS EXPOSED TO the same environment acclimate in different ways according to personal inclination. The relationship between self-realization and self-preservation varies and one must sacrifice some features of mentality to function in the world. One can wish for a different world but life depends on the way things are. For one the world is insurmountable, for another it is an opportunity. One seeks a route of escape, the other, conciliation or confrontation. And so we see adaptation to a wider social environment is necessary.

The conceptual world beyond immediate sensibility—work, family— is also a perception. However, the constraints on objects are looser and our habits, values and experiences play a greater role. One might suppose there are layers of sensibility: first, perceptual immediacy that determines the direct contact with the world; then, perception more profoundly informed by meaning and experience. The perception of a group of benign strangers will not, necessarily, activate experiential memory to the extent that members of a gang, a family or a workplace would. The variation in (the meaning of a) perception and the response to what is perceived are not secondary adjustments. This process provides opportunities for creative renewal in which valuations induce actions and re-animate the dead objects of a distant and immediate past.

There can never be a sense of equality that is not mandated by an elite or a sense of inequality with those who issue the mandate. The only viable natural system is when the varied attributes of personality—given a tolerance of difference and an abolition of unfair obstacles—settle at some level consistent with ability, with inequality relating to merit, ambition, accomplishment, and the acceptance of quality of life as outcomes of whatever gifts are in play. Aristotle wrote of constitutive luck—good health, a supportive family, native intelligence—which, along with the absence of bad luck, implies that the promise of equality is a sham.

Is it human nature, or an evolutionary trait passed on from ape-like ancestors, to need a leader and to submit to authority? Or is it militancy, persuasion or herd mentality that leads us to do so? Do bonds of dependency established in infancy continue into the social arena?

While success depends on individuality, survival (or adaptive success) depends on the immersion of individuality in a group; a fish in a school, a wolf in a pack. Withdrawal to a category may be advantageous, but remaining in the category and assimilating to others diverts self-interest so as not to provide a wedge against aggregation or servility. This is seen in interests, sports, friendships, but especially in cults, religious orders or political movements. Commonly, there is an ebb and flow of the subordinate and the self-realized. A decision that feels obligated may permit a surrender of autonomy to authority. Perhaps self-realization accompanied by autonomy comes as a shock. This shock is the seed of apartness and the ground of alienation. Submission to others attempts to establish bonds of otherness, while self-realization is the tension of category and individuality.

※

The subject/object divide, petrified as a thing-like fact in social discourse, is relaxed for novel objects to arise from a subjective ground.

The child who rebels against his parents will only sacrifice his independence to another.

If you can't decide, others will decide for you, and little by little you will disappear.

She made everyday decisions, leaving the big ones to me, but the accumulation of everyday choices choked the scarcity of major ones. Ultimately, it was her life, not mine, that I was living.

The population dynamic of evolution will always be a constraint on individuality.

Even the marginal and most eccentric seek like-minded others.

Solitude is the soil from which great oaks grow

Too frequent an appearance of the tawdry self does not, as hoped, pave the way for a beneficent one, but threatens to become the genuine in character.

Adapting to Society

Character is the sum of all selves minus the sum of all acts.

Be yourself, if you can stand it.

Are constraints on self-realization part of the self or extrinsic brakes on conduct?

Globalization and Cultural Identity

It is not emulation of the west or open borders that matter.
What counts is a mind without borders and
values that transcend locality.

THE GREAT PARADOX OF globalization is that so many people who up until now have been poorly educated or misinformed have finally gained access to a diversity of ideas and information yet they show a persistent—even in some cases increasing—tunnel vision of belief and custom. This is as if the information not only failed to bring about a greater openness but had the opposite effect, of reinforcing a more restrictive vision of the world. The database of the internet and the trafficking of ideas impels a kind of virtual multiculturalism, but its concrete realization is observed in the mixing of cultures and porous borders that bring the "global village" to a flashpoint in everyday life.

A notable example is the assimilation of newcomers with beliefs and customs that are inhospitable to those of the host culture. This problem is not, inevitably, the result of bias or lack of education. Life in a third world country, or a ghetto in a modern society, offers an island of safety and friendship, a common language, work, traditional food and clothing and religious centers. It is not the village or ghetto alone that fosters insularity, but tradition, religion, the impact of education on children and the degree of access to a wider and more cosmopolitan society. There can be openness to newcomers yet the newcomers can be resistant on an individual and societal level. A host community must decide whether to force an influx to adapt, or stand by helplessly as its values are eroded. Traditions tend to be weakened on both sides to the degree that assimilation is successful.

A sense of endangerment arises from the fear that uniformity is a greater threat to a culture than obstacles to assimilation. Personally, I am aware of feeling "more American" when I am abroad than when I am at home. The sense of apartness heightens what is authentic in the personality, which then relaxes in a return to the familiar. Identity can disperse into an alien culture or decant to a comfortable stereotype. Think how anti-Semitism forged Jewish cohesion and, conversely, its dilution with a reduction of threat. Some traditions are defended with a vigor that is explicable only by the timid indulgence of near-pathological claims for uniqueness. Was the justification of Black English not a roadblock for blacks scrambling out of poverty? The hijab of Muslim women, the yarmulke of Jews, the skull caps of the church patriots are all emblems of separateness, trivial symbols not worth fighting over. Identity in a social, parental, economic, religious, fraternal, tribal group reinforces a narrow sense of self and excludes those outside a privileged circle. It merely extends the sphere of autonomy to like-minded others.

Eccentricity is an individual value to be cherished; custom is group habit that ordinarily merits little admiration. Identity—as an inner sense of self—needs no artifice of practice or clothing. If assimilation is to be successful, outdated mythologies should be shed like old skin. The features that define an ethnic group, to the extent they encourage apartness, should ultimately be discarded; those of religion should aspire to the god of the philosophers. The quibble over what traditions to preserve or abandon avoids the deeper question of how to adapt to a new culture without relinquishing one's own customs. Like Buddhist monks who chant prayers they do not understand, the origins and meanings of most customs have been forgotten by the masses who celebrate them. The real question is, where does the feeling of identity lie, in a locality of belief, religion and/or community, in an individual self-concept or in engagement with the wider world of humanity?

The most common factors that tip the balance between adaptation and ethnicity are historical trends and most importantly the nature of the human mind itself. The expectation that global access lessens provincialism in rational decision-making is far from the truth. Ideas arise from unconscious presuppositions that assimilate information to fit underlying beliefs. Every idea is hostage to an unconscious value. Truth is ignored and subterfuges used, Schopenhauer wrote, to save a preconceived opinion or not wound a favorite idea (letter to Goethe, Nov. 11, 1815). Probity is the antidote that reason recommends but reason is often powerless against unconscious belief. To be reasonable is possible only for reasonable people. We want to believe that reason can overcome passion but more often it only reinforces an impersonal mode of thought in those predisposed to be fair-minded.

The instinctual repertoire is fundamentally selfish with other-directed acts sacrificed only when determined as necessary for individual or group survival. Ego- and exocentric trends condition the conflicts of self and other. In maturity, as others come to be apprehended as adjuncts to the self, the merit in unselfish acts may come to play a greater role in behavior.

In prior works, I discussed the prosaic need for an early infiltration of values that diminishes competition over cooperation, encourages community over individuality and promotes a humanism grounded in unselfish conduct. The installation of such values in the young is itself a value that can only be inculcated with widespread support. But even here one finds a tension between the rigid disciplines of education and the extolment of openness and flexibility. A parent wants a child to be independent and self-reliant and at the same time responsible and caring, a balance between the empathy of participation, the individuality of success, and the impersonality necessary for tolerance.

Everywhere one sees people in separate conversations on cell phones, listening to iPods on the Metro, cars that speak to drivers and machines that say "thank you". The holy grail of the communications industry is interconnectedness, but its effect is often greater isolation. What is missing is an understanding of the place of the other in the mental life. Automation and computer brains give an illusion of agency and consciousness without identity or belongingness. The utilitarian ethic and scientific calculus of mechanistic science are precisely the wrong sensitivity for a truly moral attitude.

A global perspective leads as often to indifference as to involvement. A true citizen of the world is not a traveler to foreign places, but one for whom engagement trumps autonomy. A well-informed individual can be a dangerous predator. A simple man who never ventures far from his village can be a paradigm of kindness and humility. The wholeness of the authentic life, the fulfillment of character in conduct, does not guarantee the direction of moral feeling. The most fundamental value, and the least comprehensible to a materialist ethic, is that others are concrete extensions of the self. A palpable feeling of mutuality entails a self in service to community. The artificial boundary of self and other can only be obliterated by genuine compassion and a profound sense of the wholeness of life. The mechanical self approaches the other by external bonds that are easily severed. The organic self has an intrinsic relation with the other as an actual part of its being. This is a truth hard to come by, harder still to feel, but a foundation on which our common existence and mutual happiness depend. The central lesson for the modern age is that humanity is the primary category of belongingness from which limited individualities arise.

∾

The unwelcome truth is that corporate investment has done more in the third-world than an endless gaggle of missionaries.

The plus and minus of globalization are the same, greater uniformity.

Cultures are preserved incestuously by protection from outside influence

The hope is that what is of universal value will remain as local cultures disappear

We need to get our priorities straight. A lost language is more precious than an endangered guppy.

We lament the disappearance of native cultures, but 99% of all species on the earth have become extinct. Yet the extinction of certain species of fungi or microorganisms, many of which have not even been described, may endanger the planet.

Every culture has a history of violence and intolerance. War and early death intensify a sense of vulnerability, which sharpens aesthetic feeling, as in Periclean Athens, Renaissance Italy or Elizabethan England. It seems one must choose between genius and perpetual peace.

To strive for what is admirable in all cultures and disown what is appalling in one's own would leave a set of universal values, not attributes of ethnicity.

Hard to have it both ways; assimilation and ethnic diversity.

In my country, uniformity in thought goes with diversity of life style.

In its indulgence of all content, the internet is neutral as to value. But some things matter more than others.

Complete openness is not a virtue. Any hateful attitude is reinforced. But what is the alternative?

An unwitnessed life is not felt as lived. Is this why every trivial action has to be described to someone on a cell phone?

The less people have to say, the more time they spend on the phone. Cell is a good term for those who reach out to others, locked in their own isolation.

On the street, a wire in the ear is all that separates banality from psychosis.

Is there not an element of hallucinated conversation in a telephone call?

Still, bonds are maintained by contact with others halfway around the world.

The virtues of a single person can serve as a template for humanity

The poison in the stew is self-interest. Find the antidote and humanity has a chance.

What will happen if we could engineer the "selfish gene"? Would an absence of self-interest translate to generosity? Even the most unselfish act arises from a core of need.

The argument for preserving native cultures requires their total isolation, even from those who study them.

Should we enclose an aboriginal community in Australia, a tribe in the Amazon or Andaman Islands for anthropological study? It does not usually go well to erase lines of separation.

The ghetto is problematic. Separation preserves the culture but isolates individuals from the wider society.

The price of assimilation is a change in belief, which is a change in identity.

Homogeneity is less in social fabric than a cognitive mean.

The melting pot eliminates the adventitious. Character liquefies, personality is frozen

When the congenitally blind regain sight, they often commit suicide. There is a lesson in this for assimilation.

In spite of diversity we all have more or less the same brain. Perhaps this should be the focus?

The infant produces the sounds of all languages, then only the mother tongue. We are prepared for universals before possibilities are eliminated.

Attention on the young and the future trumps past loyalties.

The virtual world of the internet competes with the virtual reality of perception. For some, a world twice removed from the real is preferable.

Sadly, the ease with which children learn to use cell phones and computers does not transfer to enjoying Beethoven and Shakespeare.

The coming-together of diversity is like an improvised dinner party that reduces to the lowest common level

People carry laptops as a surrogate brain, unaware they may forget how to use the one they were born with.

An ordinary child on the internet is a prodigy of useless learning

The more books there are on Google, the less people read them

Wholeness and Alienation

*Togetherness takes the sting out of alienation but requires
a subtraction of personality*

THERE IS NO ONE source of alienation, but all its sources have in common the sense of incompleteness or separation. The marginalization of the self as an object is in relation to others, such that it severs our connection to the community. We see this in the objectification that leaves behind subjective antecedents, such that the inner life is lost in the becoming to an object; we see this in the actualization of a self that is constrained by a surround that requires the individual to satisfy the needs of others but not his own. We sense this most deeply when we are alienated from what we intuit as the genuine self, in that the realization of an individuality entails loss of commonality with others as with the core self. Individuality places the self in conflict with convention, while in conformity the self fails to realize its potential and becomes an object among many. There is no escape from apartness.

Conversely, the feeling of incompleteness as alienation leads us to search within for what is genuine, and to explore activities and seek others that will receive, express and/or satisfy the longing of the self for wholeness, since the actualized self will realize a fraction of its potential, and completeness is ameliorated, not fulfilled in harmony with others. All attempts to alleviate alienation are bound to fail, while those designed to exploit it may succeed. This is accentuated by the fact that the wholeness of the preliminary is virtual, and does not exist or become real until it actualizes, at which point a momentary state, a brief existent, is still a fragmentary portion of the individual.

The alienation that is postulated to occur in the separation of self and world is bridged when the world lapses to its categorical underpinnings or the self apprehends the subjective quality of what appears as external reality. The individual has a choice, to act as a subject—thoughtful, contemplative, enjoying the solitary pleasures of love and other feelings—or to succumb to external circumstances, and live as a generic object, devoid of individual purpose and will. This results in the individual being a part-object in a social or political group, class, cult.

Alienation is not ordinarily a personal judgment of the objective self, the self-in-the-world. A person who is unhappy or aggrieved with his situation may feel alienated but this does not imply an objectified self that is evaluated by a more authentic one. The feeling of alienation is an internal state of frustration or despair—think of Thoreau's "quiet desperation"—that is more likely an emotional response to poor choices, bitterness over impediments or missed opportunities. The self as a commodity for others is a compromise of risk and safety, adventure and concession.

Only the final actuality—an act, object, thought—along with phases in its derivation, can be said to exist, since the preliminary, as potential or category, is non-existent until an act is realized. An implication of this account is the absence of conflict between entities postulated in the unconscious. Once a trend in thought actualizes, it no longer partakes of the furnace of unconscious cognition. Conscious ideas cannot be re-inserted into unconscious phases. The precursors of those ideas, being virtual, are without content or properties other than the most general attributes that define the category. Unconscious conflict is the tension that is transmitted when some content resolves, and is felt, in consciousness, as incomplete and therefore an unsatisfying outcome of the unconscious series. It is likely that affective tonality plays a role as to which items resolve. Intense affect is linked to preliminary cognition, and may prevent conceptual forms from realizing a more quiescent conscious phase by way of the state-specificity of the emotional tonality. Since the category/potential behind every act is always wider than the act itself, the feeling of inadequacy is a more or less constant companion of every final state. This is why we cannot identify unconscious contents in conflict, or assume conflict among contents, while competing contents that are conscious are the basis of indecision.

What is felt in the conscious subject is indecision as to competing choices. This indicates retarded (neotenous) segments in the specification, not necessarily incompleteness since a multiplicity of conscious choices may more fully deplete the potential that would be tied to only one. Also, the agency in decision contributes to self-empowerment, even if the self does not know what to do. What leads to a sense of incompleteness is the feeling of options unborn, possible selves unrealized that compete with that which actualizes. The feeling of potential sacrificed in the empirical self with the individuation of particulars is true of every entity that emerges. Wholeness ruptures in the sampling of a concept, with alienation a mismatch of actuality and possibility, and an inevitable consequence of self-realization.

Indecision can be interpreted as conflict, but not the unconscious conflict postulated by psychoanalysis. It is uncertainty as to the best or most sensible choice, taking into account the nature of the person and the external situation. The act is displaced through spontaneity in the world to uncertainty in the mind. Ultimately, a final decision is more likely to be determined by emotion than by judgment, suggesting that the option with the stronger feeling will prevail. Moreover, the thoughtful person will always find something to question in every act of thought. What might have been said or done? What if the outcome had been otherwise? Multiple perspectives do not necessarily impede choice but there is greater irresolution.

The illusion of deeper thought may compensate for the lack of decisiveness, but again there is a basis for alienation in the comparison of acts that occur spontaneously as a direct reflection of character with those that follow reflection as an excuse for irresolution. The former feel more authentic and closer to the core self, to values and beliefs, the latter, through conscious deliberation, enhance volitional feeling even though the self is forked into two or more possible routes of implementation. A self that is afflicted with a lack of wholeness, regardless of choices, will have a "what if" effect that weakens resolve.

The distinction between the spontaneous and the deliberative relates to that of unconscious and conscious, or instinctive and rational. Every conscious decision is a reinstatement of agency or a failure of assertiveness. Reflection, contemplation, deliberation, are what make us human, but the price of reason and conscious thought is distance from the primitive instigation of the mental state, which is then left behind. An affliction of instinct is the curse of reason, one of many sources of doubt, a sickness of mind or a unity of psyche.

To think and to decide is to reach finality without conviction. Conviction is like an unshakeable faith. Freud said to a young man uncertain about getting married that such decisions should come from the heart, not the head. Allow feeling to propel choice, not rational judgment, which engenders an occasion of doubt that contributes to alienation. Excess deliberation sunders the wholeness of certainty. It can also result in a life lived

Reflections on Mind and the Image of Reality

in the mind, not in the world, a life of response, not initiation, a spectator, not a participant, a retreat to mind from life itself. Wagner wrote, even after a tempestuous life, that having passed through life to the other side, he had missed life itself. No matter how accomplished and stimulating a life, the sense of dissatisfaction is a longing for a life other than, or complementary to, that which was lived.

∽

The writer hopes his books will live the life he envies in his study

There is pathos for the writer who, a poor ventriloquist, reads to a public from his latest work as if his creations are more real than he is.

The works are compensations for what is lacking in the author, but once externalized, they do not add to wholeness but deplete it.

At times of grave vulnerability I could not decide whether to walk first with my left or right foot. A morbid introspection led to paralysis for the most automatic of acts.

A life in the mind, a life in the world, a life as a compromise; one cannot avoid incompleteness.

The more eccentric a person and the more particular the personality, the greater the exclusion from others who, less differentiated, swim like fish in schools of instinctual automaticity.

Eccentricity is one way to defy conformity. Confronting or rising above it is another.

The desire to be one with my actions (Rilke) is shattered just by thinking about it.

I peer out at the world from a safe harbor of thought, scrutinize and dissect, acts of others and my own, the inner intensity of an unreal life, one of concepts, not objects, detachment, not engagement, things becoming thoughts, thoughts becoming the things one thinks about, a dream of ideas that matter more than events, originality of thought taking precedence over the novelty of the occasions to which it refers, a personal world—a psychic phantom—more real than the natural one, more immediate if less palpable, filled with meanings extracted from contingency.

> To act or act not,
> To shoot or be shot,
> Tied in a knot,
> A radical spot.

Dissent is assertion that, right or wrong, palliates the inertia of concession.

Inaction may be the soundest course but too often it strips away manhood.

We savor the inner life in the anticipation of a lover. Why not on all occasions?

The breadth of contemplation is violated by the blinders of commitment.

Think of the vulnerability of the crab when it goes naked to find a new home

The paradox is that unfilled time passes slowly but, on reflection, seems to have passed quickly, while with filled time it is the reverse.

The call of the wild

Think you can renounce the earth for higher ground? Think again.

CAN WE LIVE IN harmony with society and with nature or must we shuttle from one world into the other in order to enjoy a respite from one world without succumbing to the other? We are addicted to culture, the comforts and opportunities of a city, but are rescued by nature from its conflicts and deceits. We are no longer equipped to survive unaided, though the appeal of living close to nature—even the refreshment of a walk in the park—speaks to a deep-set animal urge that resists acculturation. This appeal is not only a longing for what many believe to be a more authentic life—the idea of the "noble savage"—but a need to dissect the layers of protection by which the native inheritance is subdued in partial expressions.

We wonder if we are surrogates of what we think we are, or who we feel we should be. We may think our life is a lie if we are not true to our genuine selves, a striving for the authenticity that more often settles on the instinctual than the acculturated. Every urge, every pain, every pleasure or bodily need, reminds us of the primeval state, the raw physical flesh of which individuals are made and the social fabric woven, especially in sexual drive, which despite its channeling into convention, or its detour in the search for love and the language of romance, uncovers the bestial in all its varied satisfactions.

The contrast is vivid. On the one hand we have the machine theory of mind and nature and, on the other, an organic theory of microgenesis in which mind and nature are living organisms. In a theory of mind as a computational network, there is continuity from mind to nature, but without value, feeling, meaning and purpose there is no prescription, much less incentive, for a way to live. Philosophy in western thought is a specialized occupation divorced from life. In contrast, in process theory, mind and nature share a common philosophy, in which a life is lived—as in Asian thought—in accordance with philosophical belief.

For me, an awareness of this commonalty led me to a country home in a farming community and a more immediate contact with the natural world. The constant astonishment of a horizon unbroken by high-rise buildings, a sky of immense blueness in day, star-clustered at night, raging storms, ferocious winds, martins on the rooftop, vipers and scorpions on the floor, sheep in the meadow, a routine like a hunter-gatherer bartering for an evening meal, herbal tea from the garden, leisure, serenity, working with one's hands, an adventure risk-free, close to nature, close to home, stirring if vicarious, far from the racket, pollution, debris, indigestibility, automation and ambitions of city life. Here one can live one moment as it rolls into the next, oblivious to all the tomorrows save for seasonal provisions. A philosophy of the present was the reality of my life.

One does not need, like Diogenes, to sleep penniless in a public bathtub to strip away the supposed artifice of civility, or like Tarzan, live a survival course in a hostile jungle. This dilemma is most intense for those in large urban centers, not for the mass of villagers who face a harsh climate and struggle to survive. They may love their natural surrounding in spite of the incessant challenge it presents, or they may feel trapped in that world, longing to escape for a life of greater comfort. It is only for the gentrified who live in relative ease and safety that a taste of nature is foie gras for the spirit, and a spectacular vista is music for the soul. Only they ask if the savagery, sublimity, wonder and diversity are not rivaled, if in some respects surpassed by human creativity. The refinement of a late Beethoven quartet is not of nature or of reason but is an other-worldly creation that exists on a higher plane. The rampant diversity that is creativity in nature, which we presume is unguided by mentality, becomes the coherent outpouring of genius in human thought.

This "call of the wild" inside us is another, perhaps the main, source of alienation. The alienation of the modern from the ancestral, the conflict of a conscious self with inner nature and a feeling of core authenticity are topics of many treatises and political tracts. Here, alienation is fully subjective, a dispute of the conscious self, compromising with the drive-based implicit self—the self of the city and the self of the Serengeti. It is less a matter of what one becomes in relation to others as who one is in relation to instinctual drive. The war of instinct with reason is a harking back to the primitive onset of the mental state from a self in which the expression of

Reflections on Mind and the Image of Reality

impulse is attenuated by habit and adaptation. The result is an individual who feels his actions are not true to his nature—unconscious and unknowable—felt in its derivation into tributaries. This feeling, combined with the derivation of content out of categories, gives a sense of multiple possibilities of realization. The anxiety is for a self that is realized as one among many possible others, with uncertainty as to which manifestation actualizes what is genuine in personality.

I do believe that one implication of this line of thought is that a society must embrace and preserve so far as possible the scale, habitats, simplicity and grandeur of nature. This inner Darwinism, which is the actualization through which an individual exists, corresponds to self-realization, but it does not replace the organic competitiveness of native behavior with the unnatural and inauthentic demands of parity and uniformity. The harmony of a society that is true to our nature can find ways to resolve the dangers and deprivations of primitive life. This does not mean priming self-preservation by menace on the metro, promoting ruthless competition or even trees springing out of cement, but rather allowing selective pressures to foster success, facilitating the cunning of the fox not the ferocity of the tiger. The struggle and violence of Darwinism is not a prescription for savage combat but a call for a compassionate meritocracy.

The cannibalism of savages takes a route through table manners to dinner at a Michelin star restaurant. Murderous rage or crime, institutionalized in war, refined in a duel or prizefight, transitions to a hostile takeover. The brutality of rape traverses prostitution to courtship. Civilization emasculates drive, withered in the parsing of categories as it passes to desire. The process of self-realization narrows to distal outcomes from immediate discharge. The tension between the potential of the core and the partiality of outcomes, the tenacity of the implicit self of drive and the surface manifold of perished objects—one recurrent and insistent, the other evanescent and malleable—leaves the individual at war with his own nature. The deep urge is exchanged for the outer appearance leaving an awareness of the resolve of recurrent nature over the tenuousness of the momentary.

∽

The sense of the divine does not come from avenues and buildings but from valleys and verdant hills.

Things of value in life are not appreciated by restless seeking but attentive immobility, the ruckus of the streets giving way to the quiet prayer of the forest

I can imagine the spirit of an old tree dancing in the moonlight, or the ghosts that haunt the houses as the friendly spirits of the wood

Can I be one with my acts in a backdrop of possibilities?

The violence of drive bubbles up to social conventions as earth's desiccated crust rises out of a volcanic core.

The light shining below (Wittgenstein) is the fire that deposits the ashes of a life

I am a piecemeal construct of acts of self-realization. The more acts recur, the more they become habitual and define who I am.

The apprehension of nature in consciousness requires the identification with nature in drive.

As a thunderous waterfall trickles into shallow streams, we are saplings stirring toward the sun but rooted in the earth.

You cannot linger in the burning light of reason without the fierce energy of drive.

The excess baggage that is not weighed when you travel is what remains even when you try to leave it behind.

Wholeness is realized when conscious will is one with instinctual drive.

Conscious deliberation is the fruit of reason but does not satisfy instinctual hunger.

Politics

Politics is the art of convincing others that personal ambition is public service

THE RELATION OF WHOLE and part in life and mind helps to explain valuation in social and political life. For example, conservatism tends to be holistic, liberalism analytic (though they often profess the opposite). The left-right brain hypothesis of Tucker, and Lakoff's proposal that conservatives are paternalistic and liberals codependent have merit, one a "vertical" hierarchy, the other "horizontal" uniformity. However, conservative values stress tradition and the social good or the welfare of community; liberal values, support change and individual rights.

We can see these tensions between individual rights and the values of community in a number of issues. For example, in the case of abortion, the fetus depends on the mother for life-support, but the mother depends on the community for survival. For the liberal, the mother is a free agent though she is just as dependent on others as the fetus is on her. The conservative professes an obligation to protect the fetus as society protects the mother. We could just as equally look at the debate over euthanasia.

On the other hand, the logic is reversed in the controversy over guns. Here we find that the safety of the community trumps the rights of individuals. Does the liberal support the right of a homeless person to defecate on his doorstep? Does the conservative believe ordinary people should have machine guns? Generally, strong opinions arise when reason is framed by belief. Because the mind cannot readily entertain competing beliefs, it takes its own beliefs to be based on reason.

Difference concerns particulars; identity involves categories. Categories cannot be identical since they have no boundaries. Categories confer identity for one object over time, not for other category members. An

Politics

ostrich and a canary are members of the same category of birds. When different people are subsumed in the same category, depending on the category, they can be treated as more or less the same, for example, Jews, Muslims.

I believe the person who slaughters a single child is no better than one who murders millions. In fact, the person who kills with his own hands may be more despicable than one who kills through intermediaries. Hitler and Jeffrey Dahmer are brothers in evil. The difference is one of scale.

From cell to tissue, from tissue to organ, from organ to organism, all depend on the *Umwelt*.

When an opportunity is missed, another may not come along, and a life may be condemned to failure. The less traveled path is an adventure in which success is less certain. However, if you choose the habitual, you are likely to feel unfulfilled. There is no-one to blame if you are risk-adverse; that is who you are. Of course, opportunities often come with conditions, straight-jackets on values, so a trade-off is always in the works

∽

If you feel exploited, turn the tables and take control. Be the author of your life. Write the script and live it

Self-hate happens when a child hates the parent it will become

A child that teases has a theory of other minds

Lovable as puppies, we take babies in our heart. But a child that loves its parents is an unexpected mercy.

Creating a job for others is nothing to applaud. It provides income, but steals a life that should have been an adventure.

Unfulfilled ambition is a common source of unhappiness but worse than no ambition at all.

Persuasion should avoid argument and focus on attitude and tendency

The odd thing about the mind is that intensity of belief is disproportionate to truth

It is a small step in false belief to delusion and conviction

Reverence for a charismatic leader depends on identification, not persuasion.

It is not what Gandhi or Mandela said that inspired; it is who they were

To change from one political party to another, if not expedience, is like a religious conversion

Reflections on Mind and the Image of Reality

> Red-handed he will claim
> Mendacity is not to blame
> If it serves a higher aim

We sacrifice mediocrity in expectation of genius, but in mind, knotty problems are left for future neuroscience, which itself needs sorting out

Mediocrity is not innocuous; it lowers the public taste for the exceptional

The well-informed are not immune to the vulgarity of unreflective opinions

When theories are in dispute, decide the matter on common sense.

Is he glib or articulate, informed or rehearsed, hard to decide what's really inside

Santayana thought history recurs for the ill-informed, but unless time is reversible, the only invariables are instinct and subjective aim

The idea of an objectified self is a metaphoric expansion of actuality. A traversal without delay through introspective and imaginative phases does not evoke options associated with the feeling of freedom. There is a presumptive loss of freedom in all objects and pursuits that carry thought forward. A free act is judged, by others, by the nature of the act, and by the agent in relation to the intention that is actualized. It seems paradoxical that spontaneity should reveal character, while deliberation is associated with the feeling of freedom. In spontaneity, the person is (free to be) what he is, opposed to the illusory freedom that comes with choice. One can deliberate and, for lack of will or confidence, or for comfort, loyalty or indebtedness, not make a free choice, like the canary that remains in the cage when the door is left open. Simple acts such as lifting a finger do not engage thought as in complex or more difficult choices in which courage is the decisive factor. For the person to feel free, thought must precede or follow the act, either as an intention or a rationale, though freedom and the feeling of free action are not the same. Agency is part of the momentary act, while action is unnecessary. One can feel volition with imagery in thought.

Any conversation that closes the door to argument is veiled propaganda

Like works of art, the uniqueness of a person increases his value

A third-person perspective deals with "input and output" and ignores internal process, reducing action and perception to machine functions. Input and output are complex evolutionary and hierarchic structures.

Think of political texts as clever displays or artful persuasions, not as truths by which to live your life. Do not be convinced by argument alone but by evidence, not by assertion but fact, not by dogma but analysis. Discard any text that does not fairly present counterpoints. The derision of opposition is an unpleasant harbinger and a mark of intolerance. Think with an open mind, look to trial and error and reach tentative conclusions. That is the right model.

A critique of technocracy overlooks the modesty with which discoveries are made.

A weak personality is changeable; a strong one is little affected by circumstance.

The more pernicious the idea, the more it is cloaked in slogans to wash over the zombie brains of followers

The just war ennobles the soldier and sets in relief the cavil, malice and pusillanimity of critics.

How many on the right or left would die for their cause as readily as a soldier throws himself on a grenade to save his comrades?

The foxhole for the courageous is the armchair of the revolutionary

For the false prophet, enmity is the disease and insurrection the cure

The unspoken context around an assertion is the sphere of its refutation

Justice and the Law

It is good that we have laws, but opportunity often lies on the cusp of illegality

MOST DECISIONS MADE BY the U. S. Supreme Court that deal with financial, social or labor issues tend to codify trends in public opinion that have outgrown prior law. These are of relatively trivial importance compared to actions of Congress and the President. If a social or religious freedom or sanction goes too far, it will usually provoke some reaction with or without the Court's intervention. Indeed, in spite of contestation and volatile arguments, decisions of the high court are less important in some respects than those of a lower judge who imposes, however justified, a death sentence or life incarceration, or dismisses a case of indisputable guilt. The former tends to be conceptual, incremental, and swayed by politics. It can be revisited and redressed. For example, affirmative action has been adjudicated many times in slightly different contexts, while the verdict made by a lower judge is for the most part irreversible.

Some decisions are not only trivial but foolish, such as a Miranda warning that hampers tactics of interrogation. If stupidity is no excuse for breaking the law, ignorance should not need a reminder. The argument that a slight procedural error should exonerate a guilty person for the sake of equal application of the law is a specious claim; a "get out of jail" card for an otherwise shaky defense. Those responsible for the error should be held to account, but unless it has a direct bearing on the crime, the law should be followed and the guilty punished.

Other decisions, such as legitimizing gay marriage, in that they are close to public consensus, pander to opinion and are largely symbolic. What is the distinction between marriage and civil union? Mind you, I see no reason to deny marriage to anyone or with any number of partners, but whatever term is used, it is still a legal contract. With the permission of the Imam, Muslims allow up to four wives so long as they are all cared for in the same way! As the old Muslim saying goes, "beat your wife regularly; if you don't know why, she does."

Decisions by the high court are justified on either an originalist or contemporary reading of the Constitution. And yet, for the most part they represent the values, presuppositions and biases of judges, who tender an outcome in which argument is window dressing. This is obvious if for no other reason than that except for egregious violations, most "hot button" issues depend on a narrow majority, so knowing the liberal or conservative bias of judges can reasonably predict their position. The only relatively objective opinions are those of little political consequence that few people care about. Perhaps the data on a case should be fed to a master computer and the results vetted by judges, possibly as a tie-breaker in an evenly divided court. Of course this would eliminate empathy, forgiveness, loyalties and personal values, but it seems the only way to ensure an unbiased opinion.

As discussed, so many of the cases to be decided concern the balance of individual freedoms with the general good, or a conflict between the religious and the secular, or State and Federal responsibility. To decide what is best for society as a whole in relation to Constitutional law is a dicey problem that for the most part results in limited opinions that can be repeatedly challenged. How many small-bore cases of religious freedom—school prayer, nativity scenes, atheism, contraceptives, reference to god—clog the Court's calendar? The exercise of religious freedom is one thing, but arguments from the point of view of a given religion should carry little weight. The same applies in other areas, such as second amendment rights for assault weapons or vigorous background checks.

The danger is that people so agitated over marginalia, unable to tolerate the slightest infringement on their belief-system or religious values, will ignore questions of greater magnitude. Most cases would disappear if people would follow the Golden Rule, live and let live, or a diluted version of the Kantian maxim.

My own view, impossible to implement, is that the high court—to be a genuinely equal branch of government—should intrude unilaterally on matters of national import. Say, instances of extra-constitutional executive power, immigration, border enforcement, economy, military intervention without a declaration of war, abusive taxation and so on, without a need for standing and without a drawn out process through the lower courts. If there is a strong objection to the Court's decision, Congress has the power to set the matter right.

The relational quality of law entails the coherence of its propositions, much as with all knowledge. We trust in the stability of such relational systems, including the world. The correspondence of a proposition or mental event with a perception, or its lack, is given in the adaptation to sensibility. The one is an intrinsic property of mind, the other, an interpretation of the passage from inner to outer in terms of a comparison of successive segments in the mental state. Coherence comes from the recurrence of the categorical underpinnings of like states, which bind objects and meanings together in an infinitely complex matrix of relations. The complexity of this background in mind, and its delimitation in correspondence, make for much uncertainty in the description of any state of affairs. Creativity occupies the inner extreme, science the outer.

∽

The law is a coherent system of relations but there is no ground on which it rests

Law lacks a solid foundation in biology or religion, depending not on logic but on values, normativity, consensus and enforcement.

The intricacy of a legal opinion does not disguise the bias that motivates it, but this is the case in all fields save perhaps mathematics.

A divided government that accomplishes little can be a blessing.

There are no great leaders, but do the times call for them?

The media should respect privacy. A leader without flaws is inauthentic.

Where is the truth in a balance of perspectives?

Punishment is the obligation of a society that defers protection to the police and outlaws personal revenge.

For those with good values, a generous reading of the ten commandments is enough

The priority of the I is cured by love for the other

Rehabilitation is successful when prisoners are incarcerated beyond the likelihood of recidivism.

An eye for an eye still makes sense. Mercy should come from the victim.

If society assumes the responsibility for justice in the name of the victim, the finality of murder obligates punishment in the extreme.

The national sport is not baseball, it is tax evasion.

Suffocate the lawyers before they suffocate us

Justice and the Law

Litigation is a weapon for those who do not want to dirty their hands

The innocent can be destroyed simply by accusation, then buried by litigation

One way to reduce the prison population is to allow the murderers to kill each other.

Attorneys are adept at moving money from one pocket to another, especially theirs

Ambiguity is the nectar of law.

For a doctor, complexity is a challenge. For a lawyer, it is an opportunity

Most people see things in black and white; the law thrives on gray.

The core of moral action is intention but the judgment of intention depends on acts. Why neutralize comparison by accusing opponents of endorsing comparable acts?

If determinism is true, punishment is for character, not responsibility. Yet those who deny free will still hope for redemption.

Malicious intent cannot be erased, only diluted by the acquisition of other-centered values.

Punishment is an obligation of a society that usurps the victim's right to restitution

They protest, rightly, if a monkey is kept in a cage, so why keep hardened, dangerous criminals in a cell for life? Whether they are eliminated or incarcerated is of little consequence. Society is no worse in either case.

Society can punish but only the victim can absolve.

The death penalty would be murder without absolute certainty of guilt. Lack of reasonable doubt is not enough.

Let's face it. By and large our society is vulgar and violent, with arrogance and strong opinion at every level, top to bottom. We need a Socratic dialectic, not only between but within individuals.

Conduct is the bridge from character to law guided by personal intent and regulated by impersonal values.

Duty

Like loyalties, duties are little morals that are the glue of society.

TO WHOM DO WE owe the obligation of duty and responsibility: to family, employer, nation or the self? The sense of duty can be exploited by those who do not feel it, avaricious children, indifferent politicians, religious zealots, and so on. For Kant, duty is the necessity to act out of reverence for the law, or according to a general maxim such as the golden rule. But without universal agreement, those who act responsibly are often vulnerable to predatory self-interest. Do unto others before they do it to you, the cynical popular version, has more pragmatic truth than a high-minded ideal. The responsible parent is at the mercy of tough-minded heirs. The honorable soldier is a pawn to a ruthless warlord.

Noble actions fulfill personal aspirations regardless of the motives of others. The soldier acts bravely even if the war is unjust or unnecessary. The loving parent divides an inheritance equally even if some are undeserving. The individual does what he believes to be the right thing irrespective of external pressures. The action comes of courage, virtue or love, but also as duty. The fact that others exploit the sense of duty does not dim its radiance, especially when the act is courageous, but casts a murky shadow on those ignoble souls who act out of selfishness and greed. This is not duty as acquiescence to law, or obedience to others, but the fulfillment or satisfaction of a belief or value that is a defining feature of character.

From the standpoint of mind-internal, duty is the realization of the values instilled by family, community and society, and reinforced by the example of others. These values are manifested in popular culture with examples in legend, stories, films and poems, from Gilgamesh to Superman, heroic figures who risk their lives for the weak. Such accounts help to reinforce courageous or unselfish acts.

Duty

Of course, duty is a two-edged sword, as in the Nazi who carries out orders. In both, the values, or "role-models" who display them, insure that the egocentric interests of the agent will not prevail. What he sees as an end may be a means to another by those to whom he is in debt. Values act as constraints on will, routing action to desired ends. This shaping effect occurs in the transition of drive, which is based on need, to desire, which is based on wish. In duty, choice is suspended, and need and wish are narrowly circumscribed to fulfill obligation.

A conflict in duty is most often a test of loyalties, not the greater good. A Muslim community that protects known terrorists places duty to faith above that to the wider society. Does public safety comes before duty to family? The father has a duty to report a criminal son to the police, but a responsibility to protect his child. To borrow a popular thought experiment, if a train could be diverted to save either three people or your child, I doubt many parents would hesitate to save their own child; unless their child is a savage criminal. The problem here is that from a qualitative standpoint all lives count the same, but one can't say, quantitatively, that three lives are worth more than one. Socrates, whose conviction was strong, placed duty to the state before the family. But would he have placed the state before the life of Plato?

And so we find frequent conflict between opposing duties or responsibilities. Should I aide my son and create dependency or let him struggle, with "tough love", and hope he comes through stronger? When does my duty to a terminal patient stop and the suspension of treatment—even assisted suicide—begin? When does tolerance give way to recrimination, sacrifice to survival? Fortunately most actions are impromptu and only problematic when under the scrutiny of self-examination. It seems unlikely we have a hierarchy of duties or obligations, but rather that choices reflect the strength of emotional predisposition and the pressures—punitive, rewarded—that drive an act forward. Fear of punishment, exclusion, condemnation, is a stronger motivation for most acts than rational judgment. In impersonal conflicts, choice is facile and guilt-free. It is chiefly when a person has divided loyalties and uncertainty about how everything will turn out that makes things hard.

For most people, the difficult choices that involve competing duties or responsibilities are settled more or less unconsciously according to the influence of tradition, filial devotion, self-confidence, ambition, fear of failure, and so on. It's a toxic stew that bubbles up to drive the person in one direction or another regardless of conscious argument. In fact, deliberation can serve less to reach a decision than to postpone it by expanding the space of the search for a better option. Finally, the decision—rational or not—is what is least dissonant to character.

⁂

Obligation entails some degree of compunction; duty entails lack of choice, responsibility is personal commitment. In all the feeling of debt weakens the feeling of coercion.

We feel duty *for* ourselves as inner necessity. Obligation *is a debt to* others. Responsibility is for others. These are degrees of imposition on free or impulsive acts.

Without a sense of duty, there is no obligation to act responsibly.

In many aspects of life, the secret of success is placing others under an obligation.

Kant's reverence for the law did not exactly lead to perpetual peace.

What is the calling of duty to those who interpret, make or enact the law? Is a higher duty involved?

The sanctity of higher law is not an appeal to religion but the deep moral truths of wisdom and experience.

Duties are not necessarily habitual, but habits are like duties to one's self.

The duty to break an unjust law comes from its unfairness, not from another law.

Responsibility depends on causal linkage that extends from the individual to the actions of others.

What does it mean to feel responsible for a wrongful act and do nothing about it? There is a debt that is not repealed by a feeling of remorse.

To carry out a duty can be to avoid thinking it through.

Lying

*If the judgment of lying depends on knowing the truth,
is lying mitigated by valuation in invested fact?*

HONOR IN LIFE AND politics is sacrificed for ambition and expediency. Examine the gain to identify the lie: something is to be accomplished. Hypocrisy always has a motive. There can be matters great and small, for pretense, for persuasion, to exact or avoid some penalty or to delude and mislead for power or influence. Every deviation from core beliefs and values is some degree of hypocrisy. A philosopher friend remarked that he never sold out, and then added, but I've never been asked. What of unrealized potential for lying or deceit? How far must one deviate from honesty to merit this appellation? The atheist who cries, Oh God, on orgasm, the pro-life woman who aborts a Down's baby, the man who professes love for a woman when he is after status or money? Is he a hypocrite or a garden-variety scoundrel?

It would be naïve to deny that there are situations when dissimulation is necessary; say when a person of solid values lies for the public good, as in the secrecy and fabrication that are essential to spies and diplomats; the ethics of collective security—in military conflict, "collateral damage"; displacement of the suffering; the sacrifice of a few for the sake of the many—are of a different order than decisions made by individuals. When an individual acts in a manner similar to a government, or applies values in foreign policy to domestic affairs, standards of personal conduct are degraded. The relation of character to conduct is the morality of individuals; the relation of conduct to law is the morality of nations.

It is unsettling that politicians adapt to shifts in circumstance by shifts in ostensible belief. Some say they have changed their views, but it would be less questionable if the change was not pandering to a constituency or in the direction of public opinion. Lying may be condemned in individuals, but hypocrisy is a norm in politics. Is this because political lying is constrained by party affiliation, or is related to a local controversy or national purpose, while personal lying has no proper justification? In the extreme, lying transcends hypocrisy and enters a sphere of pathology, as mythomania or Munchausen syndrome, in which individuals invent occasions of experience, even a fraudulent life. In those who come to believe their dissimulations, as in delusion, where belief and behavior are united, a dissociation of conscious belief and overt action is missing. I suppose one could say the absence of a fixed belief, or the failure to instill values early in life, creates a void to be filled by beliefs adapted to the immediate situation where conduct depends on external events rather than internal values.

Lying has become acceptable in public life. The decay of personal values and character in public officials and absence of shame allow hypocrites and toadies to prevail. Lying is a means to an end, a utilitarian strategy, but the cost is self-debasement and an adulteration of social morality. Lying can be a tactical maneuver or dissociation from a fundamental belief. There is honesty, if not truth, when a false belief is implemented, but not when deception and manipulation are tools for success. Truth-seeking is displaced from fact to effect, from judgment to efficacy, from the morality of character to personal advantage. Better and worse replace right and wrong; while impersonal judgment is replaced by cynical opportunism.

On the other hand it is clear that there are no evolutionary imperatives to tell the truth. In fact, organic nature is replete with examples of disguise, mimicry, bluff, entrapment, all aimed at finding a meal or avoiding predation. We are conditioned for deception, although in animals this is the essence of their being, not a departure from truth or fairness. If we are designed for deceit, honesty is an acquired trait that can be inconsistent with personal advantage. The morality of nature is survival at all costs with rare instances of questionable altruism. In humans, the object of moral concern is the other, ideally a stranger with no personal ties to the agent. One could say that individuals who act in the interest of impersonal others go against—and this is why they are anointed and admired—the fundamentally egocentric nature of the genetic endowment.

∾

The deception of animals is authentic. Could we say a chronic liar is true to his nature?

LYING

Wittgenstein said he decided on philosophy when as a boy he realized he could get more by lying than telling the truth. What makes one person use this insight to lie and another to value truth?

Exaggeration is lying with intent and conscious deviation from fact

The lies of a statesman require a different justification than those of an individual.

If practice makes perfect, an accumulation of lies fine-tunes the facility of lying.

Kant said philosophy was his mistress. Good thing, he didn't have to lie about it

Does lying imply lack of respect for public judgment or lack of constraints on truth?

No need to defer the truth or resort to "white lies" to avoid hurt. There is a middle ground

If truth is an absolute, so is a lie, but most truths, like lies, are not absolute

Is a half-truth an incomplete truth or a half-lie?

Is a partial truth a lie? What about an elaboration, an omission?

What if someone prefers flattery to truth? Does kindness excuse lying?

A person says one thing and later the opposite. How can one know if this is a lie or a shift in belief?

The dissociation is not only between what is said and what is believed, or consciousness of truth and falsehood, or action and utterance, but character and expectation.

If there is a potential for multiple versions of the self, what is the response to the "honest self" and the "dishonest self"? That is, does a liar have to be consistent in lying as an honest man is in truth?

What is the difference between telling a person they are attractive to lift their spirits, or saying nothing but thinking how plain and unattractive they are? Does lying depend on its effects?

When is the truth vicious and a lie an act of generosity? If one speaks or thinks an unpleasant truth about someone else, is there not an obligation to do the same for one's self?

We can know another person better than ourselves. With the other, we can be "objective". With ourselves, we pretend.

We can't face the truth about ourselves because we cannot know what the truth is, yet we have the right to judge others.

Is pretending to be what we are not a compensatory reaction, a state of denial or lying?

If the dishonest person acts out of unconscious bias, how do we judge a liar, and why do we praise honesty? These are marks of character which the individual is largely helpless to redress.

If action is motivated by need not desire, if needs are mostly unconscious, and if acts and utterances arise in instinct, does lying satisfy a need to which knowledge is powerless to confront? That is, the judgment of lying refers to an unconscious need that cannot be readily vetoed by consciousness of truth.

If do unto others means overlooking faults, is this lying?

The pretense of the actor is excused by knowledge of the context. This does not excuse the con man who is also playing a role. So, lying also depends on the beliefs of others.

There is a penumbra of context around every truth and lie.

Why do people apologize for mistakes even when they are intentional, but rarely for lies?

The vulnerability of a statement is often better exposed by a question than an argument.

Cosmetic surgery is a deception but is it a lie? We might say, the body does not lie. But in someone with surgery to enhance or rejuvenate appearance, is bodily change dishonest? How does this differ from adding makeup, attractive clothing, concealing defects? On the other hand, full disclosure can be repellant.

Character and personality

SINCE ARISTOTLE, CHARACTER HAS been described in moral terms, such as good or bad, referring to what is abiding, stable and predictable in behavior, or perhaps the mean of one's acts independent to an extent of social activity. Such qualities as courageous, timid, compassionate, are assigned to character, while personality depends for the most part on a social judgment, as in charming, aloof, unpleasant. This implies a deeper origin of character, and a more superficial source of personality, though the former is largely acquired and the latter has innate determinants. While character is a "could not have done otherwise", personality can be feigned. A courageous person is not timid but a cheerful one has despondent periods. Character persists behind the ephemeral, engaging the habitual values that underlie changing circumstance. One could say, character is aligned with the "me", personality with the "I".

Character reflects core tendencies in relation to values and beliefs, while personality is the empirical self of the occasion, a self that accommodates to others, that is driven by whim and sensibility and, in spite of innate factors, is closer to the world surface. Character is tacit and relatively uniform across occasions. A courageous person will show courage regardless of the danger or the actions of others. While courage may not be rational, it is not immune to reason. The courageous will not risk it all for a trivial, futile or foolhardy venture, so that an implicit judgment of the risk/benefit ratio is involved. In contrast, a cheerful personality will be affected by social interaction. There is some overlap, as when cheerfulness in a perilous situation can be a mark of courage, or when courage is posturing or a display of vanity. Personality is framed by character, which is the originating tendency.

If character is the sum of one's acts, personality is the individuality of response to the range and diversity of instances. Ordinarily, we judge character by action over occurrences. A person who affects kindness in one situation may show meanness in another. We might then say his character is variable or attendant on mood or conditions. Consider someone who harbors racist beliefs that are maintained in secrecy. To unearth such attitudes would impugn his character, but if he never expressed such beliefs, a judgment of character might be mistaken. This raises the question of whether actions are essential to such a judgment, but if one can dissimulate convincingly over time, such judgments will be inaccurate. There is also a psychoanalytic perspective in which a trait or behavior, such as generosity, is seen as a compensation for guilt over some prior experience, a diversion from a more basic miserliness, or as an inducement for personal gain. Occasionally, character undergoes change when different values are assimilated—moral, religious—as in the possibility of salvation, rehabilitation or redemption, but personality is difficult to alter. A morose or shy individual can hardly be the life of the party, while an outgoing or obstreperous one will have difficulty showing restraint.

Character is not homogeneous, since competing values are engaged and the right thing to do is not always evident. Conscience is the friction of positive valuations with a dubious course of potential or actual behavior, while remorse is its affective tonality.

Character is revealed in spontaneous acts, though reflection prior to decision also discloses character but of a different type; one is impulsive, the other deliberative, even if outcomes are identical.

A recurrent, and particularly contemporary, problem is the sacrifice of values that make for a good or honorable character when self-serving goals are better achieved by pretense. The common dissemblance of outer charm to advance selfish goals implies that character is better displayed in solitary acts.

Personality is in the service of character but not the reverse.

A person of good character will act to foster goodness and honesty, while a defective or deceitful character can manipulate personality to achieve aims that would clash with positive valuations. Good or bad character has a different effect on personality, the former as a constraint, the latter as a goad.

∽

Values not grounded in absolutes allow expediency to dominate, guided by acquisition.

The subjection of conduct to law constrains intent, which is the parsing of character to conduct.

The cynic attacks a good character more readily than a pleasing personality, since it is easier to apply selfish motives to goodness than to affability.

Character is less resistant to the influence of societal valuations.

A tension of values is a search for action that satisfies the demands of character without sacrificing the needs of personality.

Values are the inner voice of character, and extend into object-valuations. This is why we say, what you choose is who you are.

In the derivation of value, the intra-psychic determines character, the extra-psychic deposits objects. Value is ineffable feeling; fact is a naked object. Feeling in character is stripped in object value

The affective tonality of the core arises in instinctual primes that are pruned to valuations.

There are greater incentives to a pleasing personality than a good character, which is under constant assault.

Change in character occurs with a replacement of values, to which personality is largely indifferent.

If we are divided *au fond*, why is character not constantly assailed by opposing impulse?

Reflection and Expectation

*What happens to the alternate histories that fail to materialize?
Do they lead to other presents and other worlds?*

IT SEEMS EVIDENT THAT the distinction between holistic and analytic thinking—typified by the difference in the (largely) German and Anglo-American schools—points to two different modes of thought. To a certain extent, they are caricatured in right and left hemisphere functions represented in neuroscience and philosophy of mind. The holistic mode seeks to delve ever more deeply into the undersurface of appearance. The analytic mode is restricted to objects, demonstration and fact ultimately giving greater importance to predictions and outcomes. Subjectivity, first-person, rationalist or intrapsychic approaches tend to seek the inner, often unconscious, ground of acts and objects; whereas objective, third-person, empiricist or extra-psychic approaches are based in behavior and object-relations. The one can lead to mystical ideation, the other to skepticism. One can reasonably assert that a significant advance will depend on a combination of both, resolving whole and part, theory and data, the general and the local, continuities among particulars and their coherence or relatedness to the foundation from which they arise. The one must climb out of the speculative well of subjective depth to the bright but messy surface of actual life, the other must descend from the multiplicity of conscious detail to its formative underpinnings, from synthesis to analysis and back.

We know scholars who begin with a limited problem and elaborate a world of relations, and those who begin with generalities and become enmeshed in a wilderness of fact. One friend began a dissertation on a play by Pirandello, postponing his defense until he mastered commentary in a dozen languages. Another, to know the historical context of his topic, a single case of Freud's, became an authority on European history. The

Reflection and Expectation

particular is not always generalized. A career can spent on a nest of cells in the brainstem or the habits of a rare species of frog. A Nobel was given for studies of the sea slug with scant application to higher organisms. The study of particulars can stop at some point in the elucidation of complexity or, perceiving universals or a wider theme, go onto further generalization. To expend time on a narrow agenda may reap reward or squander a life.

In continental philosophy, the proliferation of a theme can leave the reader spellbound by the erudition and extravagance of associations, which migrate far from matters at hand, while the circumnavigation avoids specificity and commitment. The context replaces the argument or, put differently, perspective is dispersed over a variety of instantiations. For some theorists, such as Slavoj Žižek, a shared predicate unites a diversity of observations—art, film, literature, neuroscience—all of which go into a bouillabaisse of a perspective essentially a web of interconnectedness in which marginal relations supplant truth with plausibility. One could say the potential in the fact, not the fact itself, is the engine of speculation

While analytic thought is predictive, with explanation based on causal outcomes, holism is retrodictive, with explanation based on antecedents. In one, the orientation is from present to future, for the other, from past to present. Retrospective theories are difficult to prove, let alone test, such as evolutionary and maturational theory, psychoanalysis and microgenesis. They rely on a preponderance of observation, coherence and, generally, an absence of a viable competing theory that conforms to the dominant paradigm. In retrodiction, there are progressively earlier stages, for example, tracing evolution back to primal slime and the transition from the material to the organic, even opening a door, in those so inclined, to divine instigation.

I would say the distinction between the subjective and objective, apart from inner and outer, becoming and being, is that one is primarily centered in concepts, the other in objects. The attraction probably corresponds to different temperaments, one comfortable with flux, the other with stasis, one with totalities, the other with particulars, one with theory (e.g. a theory of everything, not only in physics but in historical, political and other fields of enquiry) the other with the study and application of salient fact to a discrete problem. Even if materialism in current science and philosophy tends to dismiss religious belief and discourse as mumbo jumbo, those dissatisfied with mere factuality and sensitive to the mystery in every demonstration will exhibit greater openness to unseen possibilities. This impulse took Newton to spiritualism and Oppenheimer to Buddhism.

Reflections on Mind and the Image of Reality

From the standpoint of the present—in science, politics and other pursuits—we reconstruct a past—yesterday or thousands of years ago—to explain how we arrived at this point. We create a story of change in one direction that eventuates in the present and accounts for current states of affairs. In doing this, we naturally omit those dead ends or marginal events that did not have a major, if any, impact on subsequent history.

∾

The great men who punctuate history are accidents of the Zeitgeist

Like byways on a journey, the footnotes are often more interesting than the text

Some mysteries science can never explain. An example is why, in spite of branching, evolution does not stop or regress but goes in a forward direction.

We think of the past as fixed but every interpretation gives a different past

History is important from the standpoint of the present as a record, but not the only record, of how we arrived at this point.

Like the charm of a scenic detour, the byways of the past are often more fascinating than the highway of historical progress.

Without god or a god's eye vision, what is the meaning of the fixity of the past? We can say it is true that a past event occurred, like the naval battle of Aristotle, but that truth depends on other events, in fact, a long causal series of before and after.

If the past does not exist, historical fact is a statement about non-existents.

We conjure up a past to account for the present, but all we have are relics: books, artifacts, memories.

The past is not a series of facts but a deliverance into the next moment.

> Footprints in the sand forgotten in the tides
> Conversations, thoughts, moods besides
> Vanish in the mist along the shore
> Existing then, but now exist no more.

Non-existents have profound effects on human action. Myth and religious fables are examples.

Does a half-cycle of a chronon exist? Does something that lasts a billionth of a second exist?

Reflection and Expectation

A poem in my head seems less real than written on paper, but still more real when published. Are degrees of realness also degrees of existence?

To say something once existed is to say every moment of the thing existed, or that a series of moments comprising the thing existed including those just before and after.

If a thing is an event, and an event is a process of change, what exactly is it of the past that exists? If a process is a transition of changes, and if things or events are bounded durations of process, in what sense do they exist?

Explanation too often is a re-statement of the problem to be explained

The unknowable is not just beyond the limits of knowledge but penetrates every fact. It does not support a specific belief but justifies a suspension of certitude.

For the mystic like Tennyson, a flower holds all the secrets of the universe. But an understanding of physics does not explain the existence of a flower

We can reduce everything to physics, but can we begin with physics and regenerate what has been reduced?

Consensus is often correct, but it is a good place to begin enquiry

It is not the fact but the value in the fact that is the kernel of discovery.

The tacit knowledge in the growth of plants surpasses the skill of the gardener.

It is not the plop of the stone in the water but the waves it creates.

The potential in an idea is sacrificed in the precision of its formulation

Observations are not facts, but facts are redundant observations.

The Marxist trend is natural to continental philosophy where arguments rest on theoretical appeal, not on demonstration.

The utopia of theory is a cure for the malaise of fact, but fact is a respite from the maze of speculation.

Why is ambiguity a clash of two perspectives? The same reason that choice narrows down to two options.

Is decision a tree of binary choices or the elicitation of an option out of background possibilities?

It is easier to swim downstream with the current than upstream to the source.

Some like to play in shallow tributaries, some in the rapids, a few in deep waters.

Reflections on Mind and the Image of Reality

> Now that he is dead
> The knowledge in his head
> Is gathered in his books
> Where no one ever looks

Learn from what is written but understand from what is taught
If people forget a novel but recall the gist, why not just write that?
Perhaps the gist is similar to the idea that precedes the actual writing.

PART IV

The Imaginative Animal

How do we distinguish the habitual from the creative?

Writing

The main thing is to find an authentic voice.
You will know it when your whole being sings one song.

WRITING HELPS ME DISCERN what I am thinking. Once I write it down, my thought becomes clear. I can revisit what I have written and judge if it is well-stated and makes sense. In conversation, my thought takes shape as I am speaking. Sometimes, when I talk to myself, thought is generated, but more often the inner monologue is the working-out of plans or possibilities. Before a thought appears I feel an inclination in its direction. The thought is not yet a presentation, not even a vague content or intuition, more a potential for an idea in one class or category. The direction crystallizes the idea as a larger or smaller whole.

A thought may be compact, such as the epigrams in this book, and then is unpacked as its compactness is fleshed out in a brief essay. Any epigram or apothegm can be expanded to an essay or a book. In my case, ideas emerge as successive wholes in stages from my pen.

Thinking is ignoring distraction while waiting for thought to come. Effort is counter-productive. A powerful theme channels thinking within its boundaries, such that the ideas that are produced will be coherent explorations or arguments for the value or validity of the idea. The theme, or core idea, is often imprecise, and does not have to be true, just one that appeals at some depth to the beliefs and interests of the individual. This can be a single word, a memory or perception. For Proust, famously, a madeleine, for Sartre, the insight—valid or not—that existence precedes essence, for Byron, perhaps a voyage to Italy, for Stoppard, a problem in philosophy.

We do not know where thoughts come from or how they arise, so we attribute the formative phases to the unconscious. These phases have been studied largely in relation to language, and mainly from a computational standpoint. In my view, the directional feeling points to the derivation of experiential memory, or of lexical-semantic and object concepts, to some category of verbal or visual meaning, which then arouses sub-categories that narrow the impending thought to a modality of realization within an ongoing trend in thinking. Finally, through the play of category-overlap, ideas precipitate in thought, speech or writing. The expansiveness of thought, which varies among individuals, depends on the spread of categories within a superordinate construct to arrive at a particular idea within a larger class or theme.

A poet may compose beautiful verse but often only a few lines are remembered. In a novel, much goes on between passages of great beauty or insight, as in life with its occasions of excitement separated by stretches of boredom. The relaxation of intensity, the tranquil unpeeling of ideas, the small touches, decorative but irrelevant to the theme are unlike a gastronomic meal in which every morsel is delicious. Much of writing is preparation, padding, bridging from one salvo to another as trenchant or witty passages arrive like shotgun pellets. Some shorter poems—say, by Keats—are a single concentrated thought with beauty in every line. The rationale for an extended work, a novel, an epic poem, is to draw the reader into an imaginary theater, as well as to display dexterity and inventiveness.

Philosophical texts must sustain a lengthy argument and yet a powerful idea, especially in the physical sciences, can be expressed in a few pages. A few important books read well are preferable to many skimmed carelessly. Naturally, an author feels each passage, even every word, is vital to the structure of the work, to transmit and fully discharge its ideas for an ideal reader. The object is to transport the reader to a real or imaginary world as an experience of a literary whole.

Sartre was said to do much of his writing at *Les Deux Magots*. I too prefer a café to a desk, a crowded beach to seclusion, a park bench to an office. Perhaps, intimidation by the friendly ghosts in my study drives me to working in the midst of a nattering public, or when fully alone, I am easily distracted; ignoring others helps to focus my mind.

༺༻

Scribble something. A blank page is terrifying.

Unlike the writer, the ordinary person is not rattled waiting for words that do not come.

Were flakes of gold lost in a river of silt?

Writing

I write more when time is limited than when I have nothing to do. Any idea why?

There comes a time in writing when a book takes on a life of its own to which my own life is subordinate.

Abandon writing and start living if not too late, though living without writing is like loving without a lover.

When to stop? It is not that I have said all I wanted to say, but after a while, fatigue sets in and life intervenes. Still, the jackets of my books are artificial boundaries in a continuous narrative.

"I sought a theme and sought for it in vain", the aging Yeats wrote. He went back to the past and produced one of his finest poems.

A theme for a poem, an essay, a work of art, is subordinate to a wider category of interest. Go into the past and it will come

To fail to find a theme is an inability to mine novel content from a category that has been visited one time too many.

There is always a wider whole behind every particular. When a theme won't come, go behind it to the deeper idea.

A reader unwilling to expend the effort of the writer is like someone strolling through a museum glancing at the paintings.

The living are busy with other things so I write for the ghosts of the dead.

In every case, the theme is nested in, and realized from, an underlying frame or concept.

On this view, the more significant influence of reading, conversation, art, is not to inculcate but to arouse, to inspire, to evoke new ideas and endeavors. To engorge and regurgitate is not thought; nor is passive enjoyment. Schopenhauer put it concisely, reading is thinking with someone else's brain.

Though a period of learning and ingestion is necessary for original thought, originality comes of fusion, displacement, condensation, metaphoric or meaning relations aroused by some aspect of the learned content.

When something learned is transformed to something new, how does the original remain unaltered? Why does it not undergo change by virtue of being incorporated in thought?

Reading Larkin inspires a new idea but still there is Larkin. Some portion of a poem goes into the idea without corrupting the poem. Similarly, memory is unaltered though it provides food for thought. What are the implications of this observation?

How could conscious or unconscious thought search unconscious memory? Memory retains its original character after recall, and does not fade. It's strength is in accordance with how often it is accessed.

Originality is not a rearrangement of content but an extraction of kernels for extrapolation to adjacent or tangential ideas.

One can be confused in memory, but when portions of a memory transfer to thought, their origin is often not clear.

Those who read for the beauty of language can miss the meanings below.

In life, art and philosophy, beauty of expression may conceal vacuity of thought.

In continental philosophy, thought is open-ended; analytic thinking seeks the essential and sheds ramifications: one is a voyage of ideas, the other, an encampment.

The essence of a thing is no more or less than what the thing is, but deciding what it is, is not an easy matter.

How is it that we can read a marvelous phrase and enjoy it without knowing what it means? There may be ideas within nonsense. There is serious thought behind *"twas brillig, and the slithy toves.*

Suppose I say, the essence of a thought is buried in its reflection in the mind of an imaginary man. Is this statement nonsense, or is it profound?

Cultural mythology

Many who are un-heroic are lost for the sake of a lone survivor.

MYTH IS A NARRATIVE mode of magical thinking that rests on the edge of the believable, not merely as a fable of fantasy and adventure or an account of origins or inexplicable nature. The objectification in myth of the inner unseen is an embodiment of the progression over phases in the mind/brain state. Examples are the origination myths that ground religions, or descriptions of the myth of the hero, a passage from innocence or unity through conflict to final transcendence, the journey through many dangers of Odysseus, the trials of the Buddha (perhaps also a mythic figure) that were a prelude to enlightenment, thematic in his disciples as in other religions, Christian sacrifice, penitence and redemption, the mortifications of the saints as necessary way-stations to achieve union with god, or as Augustine put it, hearts that are restless until they rest in Thee.

The traversal from unconscious instinct to conscious simplicity is a mythic journey that conforms to phases in the actualization of the mental state. The violation of physical laws of time and space in myth mirrors the timelessness or simultaneity of the unconscious prior to succession in time; the fluid volumetric space of dream and myth anticipates the becoming of a communal Euclidean space.

Myth is close to spirit, to subjectivity, animism and unconscious mind, with objectivity conceived not as a world distinct from mind but as an outcome that fulfills a subjective aim and satisfies a narrative goal. In its simplest form, the hero leaves the innocence (animal nature) of the herd or hearth to confront and conquer various dangers—demons, giants, dragons—to achieve fame and marry a fair lady. The drama is a personification of evolutionary mentality, a passage in mind through "unreal" dangers, i.e. the potential for error or elimination, to achieve a higher actuality or nobler state of existence that is based in convention and reality. Combat, struggle and triumph are objectifications in human terms of the implicit sculpting of potential competitors in the specification of conscious data. A precise recapitulation of the trajectory of mind, like stages of mythic transition, is more or less repeated in every maturational history.

The fairytale also contains features of a cultural mythology but in the form of a story for children. As Betlheim noted, the fairy tale dramatizes anxieties and unconscious fears in the natural course of development. Cinderella's slipper—the fit of a member in a sheath—is a clear forecast of the sexual fear attached to the wedding night, the excitement and trauma of violation, the bloody penetration (like an avenging sword), the rupture of virginity, are the female equivalent of a contest with dragons that is a rite of manhood in boys. A similar interpretation applies to the rapacious wolf in Little Red Riding Hood, the witch in Snow White and Rapunzel—the self-evident symbolism of the tower—stories that illustrate a rite of passage for the young girl from purity, innocence and the simplicity of animal mind, through conflict, trauma and uncertainty of elimination or annihilation. The emphasis here is not on the often far-fetched symbolism of Freud, in which everything is a symbol of something else, but on the recurrence in an act of cognition of a passage to conscious knowledge through phases in which an actuality is derived by a parsing of possible others.

Adventure films and stories that have a beginning, middle and end, resemble coming-of-age fables and myths. In the formulaic Western epic, a peaceful stranger manages to single-handedly defeat a desperado or savage band of killers. The hero who often rides off in the sunset, disappearing as when he magically appeared, is a fitting conclusion to the unreal incarnation of unconscious process. The crime story touches on the same theme, with the heroic detective, often a loner or outcast, overcoming personal conflicts, who faces alone the schemes and threats of dangerous antagonists—a crime boss, mafia don or just a mad killer (though in these instances it is often the fallen hero who repeats a perilous journey rather than the working-through of innocence). Such dramas show that the heroic journey is not a single encounter but an enactment and recurrence of the mental state. As in life, the hero remains heroic through repeated acts of heroism. The moral dimension in all heroic tales is the battle of good and evil and the triumph of goodness and courage.

It could be said that this progression occurs in other fields such as in pure music, which often begins with a simple opening theme that undergoes a wandering, an elaboration or variations, at times dissonance, until tension is resolved, say by a return to the tonic or tonal center of the piece. In works of musical genius the mental process of the composer can be heard in the music he composes. Similarly, the writer in the act of writing displays the same creative process. This is also the story of the creative act that repeatedly descends to the unconscious, like Orpheus to the underworld, to retrieve images of power in sub-surface turbulence and carry them to coherence and conscious representation.

The mythic adventure coincides with the urge to autonomy, or an assertion of separation out of dependency, as with a resolution of the subjective into veridical fact. The pressure to individuality is aligned with the object-formation, i.e. the surge from whole to part or the impulse to analysis in order to achieve detachment from the subjective and intra-psychic. The passage from generality to precision, from category to item, so far as it involves a suppression of alternatives, is played out in art and myth as an individuation of conscious states from the furnace of creative thought.

We are all potential myth-makers. There is a tendency to see one's own life in mythic perspective, enhancing obstacles and glorifying their overcoming. Parents can take on magical attributes opaque to a neutral observer. One sees this tendency in the child's wish to be the center of the bedtime stories parents tell to them. For many children, parents are the dragons against which they struggle. Or perhaps the dragons are the parents in disguise.

᠅

The pedestrian antics of the rebellious teenager re-enact a common mythic history in the relative safety of family life, with often petty conflicts magnified to crises that seek resolution.

In modern life, as in myth, the traversal through adversity can be largely imaginary but the cost of failure is elimination from competitive achievement.

To join a mob or gang is to abandon solitary adventure for safety in a pack. The gang is then the adversary the hero must confront.

Those who do not complete the mythic journey in one form or another are left behind or destined to repeat it.

When meaning extracted from near-lethal experience, in sport, travel, military life or elsewhere does not satisfy the subjective aim, danger can become intoxicating.

Judge by appearance but keep an eye on the unseen.

The criminal who sinks to ignoble means cannot resolve or rise above them.

Evil as a response to good is a false path to the heroic.

Art and Philosophy

Philosophy approaches art when every portion of the canvas is filled in

HERE I WANT TO discuss awareness in a different sense, that of someone who is acutely aware of, or sensitive to, the feelings and responses of others and the environment, awareness as an unusual openness to living nature and social organism, and retention even of the minutiae of momentary experience. The best examples are those writers who give detailed, often exquisite, descriptions of the sights and sounds around them, those with an exceptional memory for the sensible, the incidental, the refined, the exotic, the mundane, the taste and presentation of a meal, the smells of the street and market, the fields, the flowers and changing seasons, the clarity of light, the obscurity of dusk, the passage of snow to water, raindrops ambling down a window, day into night, a leaf, a star, varieties of dress and decoration, the sound of a voice, the subtle moods of an acquaintance or lover, those writers who can bring to life—more vividly than in life—a world of observation that for many goes largely unnoticed.

I believe this owes to a greater receptiveness on the side of sensibility—perhaps in the way an animal is acutely aware of its surround—an almost preternatural delight in the fine-grain of experience that is informed by taste and imagination. The fundamental difference between those largely oblivious to the richness of the external and those enraptured by it is that the latter have an eruption of object-feeling that goes into the world as an intense valuation of its multiplicity, while the former have an emotional life that is submerged, attached to wholes and perhaps derailed or of lower amplitude. The capacity to revel in the external is common enough, especially in certain professions such as decorative arts, fashion, connoisseurship, antiquities, photography and the like, but the ability to revive and rework experience in the imagination in pursuit of an original subjective aim is the creative gift.

Naturally, a successful artist must—in painting, literature or music—transmit to others not only emotion but ideas, a view of life or personal philosophy. The philosopher, though avoiding beauty in expression for its own sake, must possess a literary flair to convey ideas with grace, fluency and economy, aiding the reader without sacrifice of complexity. When philosophy aspires to literature, the result is ancillary digression—kernels of thought buried in haystacks—while in literature that is too philosophical the impulse to generate description at the surface, however elegant, gives a patina of seriousness that encircles but never seizes the revelation to which it aspires.

At its best, philosophy deepens and expands the theme of an argument, avoiding the adventitious, while literature creates portraits in words to evoke an auditory or verbal image of sensitivity and beauty, or a visual image of an individual life and time. Literature can inform philosophy, and the reverse, but literary philosophy substitutes expansiveness just when depth and concision are required, with no one section more important than the entirety of the work. This is comparable to a philosophical art-work that replaces the concrete with the abstract. In doing so, the philosophical intent dims the feeling that art-works should convey, so to say squeezing the vital juices of emotion from the fruits of lifeless knowledge.

One could say the artist has an acute awareness of external impressions that are incorporated in memory and the creative imagination, while the philosopher has an unusual access to mind-internal and rational ideation, foregoing imaginative excess for the appeal of the veritable. Wide knowledge enhances art and philosophy, but in art the personal experience—avoided in science and philosophy—is paramount. There is generally a different engagement with life. The impact of impressions in the artist arouses a hunger for more, while the philosopher retreats from the external and its distractions to better focus on mind-internal. Too great a thirst for life can lead to an intellectual drought, while an artist who bathes in the cold depths of philosophy loses contact with the very essence of an artwork. It is a matter of degree, one beginning with the material of life, the other with theoretical claims on the nature of this material and, at least historically, a continuity of the concrete data of art with the abstract categories of philosophy.

Art and Philosophy

While an artist may succumb to the harsh world of drugs and alcohol, the philosopher descends to a psychic pit of moodiness and depression.

Of an absent-minded professor, James said he was present-minded somewhere else. Thought provides the experience that is lost in detachment.

Seduction forgets the idea for the sake of the object, while love carries the object back to the idea.

It is not a choice of concept or object. Apart, they cannot exist.

> Hoping that an idea would come
> I missed the wisteria in full bloom

There is beauty in ugliness as evil in the heart of goodness. To see this, we need to go beneath surface appearance.

Hungry for a new idea? Feast on nature and perhaps it will come.

Why unity if not to discharge it? Why diversity if not to enjoy it?

The perishing is part of the replacing. Mind and nature grow from decrepitude.

When one day my world, not yours, disappears, will my ideas, no less real, live on?

Science advances among peers, art is a triumph of the individual.

Creativity[1]

Every creative person wants a fresh creation,
but one genuinely new idea is rare enough

MUCH HAS BEEN WRITTEN on the development and character of the creative personality, but little on the mental process underlying creative thought. Degree and quality of inexactness in replication allows for novelty and helps to explain innovation, originality and creative genius. I believe this to be an exaggeration and propagation of the whole/part or category/member relation essential to the formation of every entity and its replication each moment. Is creativity just a re-arrangement of pre-existing elements or does it bring the genuinely new into existence? If the latter, creativity would be a strong rebuke to the inadequacy of causal theory. Transition in mind and world is a uniform process of continuous novelty. Creativity varies in domain and power and, in the prepared mind, in relation to experience. It is an intermittent enhancement of the universal novelty that is the basis of change by way of whole/part shifts in the recurrence of every organism and entity.

∽

Careful what you read. If you open your brain to others, you may think their thoughts are yours.

A world without Brahms, an endless winter of Norwegian darkness; a world without Schubert, the birds fail to sing. A world without Beethoven is silent as the moon

When Beethoven revised a musical idea, inspiration made the choice

Who except Beethoven could say that Beethoven should have done otherwise?

---

1. See Brown (2017) *Metapsychology of the Creative Process*. Imprint Academic, Exeter

CREATIVITY

The creative requires incitement from below, not regulation from above

The fantasy that is essential to the creative is an exploration of novelty. Education kills the creative more than it inspires it

The goal of a society that values freedom, art and culture is liberation from habit and coercion

Great art is the satisfaction of a totality, a unified thought; it does not point beyond itself

A poem should be, not mean, wrote MacLeish, capturing this sentiment

In a world of ideas, theory has precedence over practice

It may work in practice but if it is theoretically unsound, change the practice not the theory. At least, this is how many bright people think.

Action enriches the creative when it stops short of finality

Art is a compromise of the real and the imaginary, or the actual and the implausible

Where is credit due if art is revelation?

Music is alive in the imagination when self and sound are one, like the feeling of the other when value returns to mind.

Art instills feeling in beauty

Love perceives beauty in feeling

When writers write about writing, is that a topic by default?

Bach composed for the glory of god. Even the atheist should work in this way

To compose for an "immortal beloved", or a muse, from Dante to Yeats, is to aim at beauty and perfection. These days, few write or compose to please god or an unconsummated love; probably, one reason we live in such mediocre times.

The good writer should know if the effect is worthy

A landscape beautiful at a distance is less so in a patch of nettles

Feeling condenses a melody to a moment in order to hear a series of tones

Every fox wants one big idea. Every hedgehog wants just one more.

Great art is in character

Superficial in personality

In commentary, the writer becomes the other as the self objectifies in words.

Reflections on Mind and the Image of Reality

Wittgenstein asked, if I write in the air am I writing in the mind or the air. Of course, in the mind

Thoughts objectify when words leave the mind to become scribbles on a page. What actually happens when a mental word is written and becomes a public object?

I feel that tearing up the page before anyone reads it preserves the privacy of the thought that gave it life. Even a published manuscript unread by others preserves the secrecy of its author. The moment a word leaves my pen it is irreversible when a moment ago it was just a thought.

If evil is the heart of goodness, what is the heart of beauty?

Science precipitates the value restored in art

Repeating the meaningless may convince others it is meaningful

The charm of metaphor is the avoidance of redundancy: its power is to vivify concepts

Instead of saying it directly, approach it from different angles. Ironically, this was the model of the tales of the devout Rabbi Nachman and the Cantos of the anti-semite Ezra Pound.

Art reclaims the personal feeling that is lost in consensual fact

Creativity in writing is not just finding the words; it is in the deletion of excess

The pencil is one part of the story, the eraser the other

I read what I have written but the writer is nowhere to be found

Sometimes I am amazed at what I have written. Someone else must be the writer. I'm just an ordinary guy

My words are fragments that point to what I mean to say

Writing is retaliation for an unfinished life, or an attempt to extend life into the minds and sympathies of others

Writing is conversation with the self as reader

Why am I depressed when a book is finished? Is it the exhaustion of the idea, the difficulty to start another, the failure of others to understand or appreciate, or the gap between what I have written and what I wanted to say?

I try to write something original but cannot escape my own writings

Artistic creation is unconscious partition and revision. Conscious effort has less efficacy than spontaneous discovery

Does the will to write keep me writing, or does weakness of will fail to stop me?

Weeds must be destroyed so the flowers will grow

CREATIVITY

How can I finish this book if I can always insert one more line?
Emptiness or surrender is not the only path to freedom
The creative is also a way to escape repetition
The restrictions that art abhors are essential to science.
An excess of caution is the graveyard of spontaneity

    What in art is meant to last
    In science is surpassed,
    The one supine at fashion's feet
    The other soon obsolete

Truth and objectivity

The difference between hypothesis and fact is evidence, but also conviction.

ALTHOUGH ALL EVENTS, THINGS and propositions are subjective, to say the objective is the outer rim of subjectivity is not to imperil truth. We speak of truth for imaginary events. It is true that a narwhale and a unicorn have one horn, but only the former is an actual object. Is the statement, "a unicorn has one horn" true even if the animal does not exist? If statements about non-existents can be true, how does that impact statements about things that do exist? Does a truth-judgment about the non-existent require a qualification? What of intermediate cases? In what sense is a dream or an idea an existent? The interpretation of a physical event can be true or false but what about dream interpretation? Even if there is consensus, does this make it true? What is needed to go from hypothesis to fact? In most fields, the more restricted the observation, the more it can be established as true. And yet, this isolates the fact from its original context which could ultimately undermine its truth.

☙

Is it the case that truth is the probability of something being true?

The clearest truths are tautologies, A is A. In logic, the conclusion is given in the premise

Jung built his theories on his dreams. What kind of foundation is that?

What does one do with facts that appear to contradict a thesis but are outside the paradigm?

What most people believe to be true is probably false, but that is not always a good place to begin.

When a hypothesis becomes true over time, was it true all along? Are most truths provisional?

Truth and Objectivity

Can argument establish truth or are data necessary?

If truth is pragmatic, value makes the final decision.

The truths that are uncovered in the elimination of possibilities, or a method of negation, are an alternative to that which is discovered by direct observation.

A truth that is felt in the beauty of exposition is closer to poetry than philosophy.

The universe inside my head is a microcosm of that outside.

The ship has not sunk but is heading for the shoals

To prove a theory is one strategy, to fail to disconfirm it is another

I do not believe there has ever been a decisive experiment in psychology. Every finding could be interpreted differently.

Once a theory is widely accepted, its refutation may require more than contradictory evidence; there must be an alternate hypothesis

An accumulation of data is more likely to flow from a theory than give rise to it.

A theory that postulates what is presently unknown is like Beethoven composing for pianos not yet invented.

The strategy is not to reduce mind to brain, and brain to physics, but to demonstrate the operation of physical law in mind/brain process.

It is less likely that the laws of mind are the basis of physical laws than the other way around, but the possibility is worth considering.

Could someone believe that physical laws—those of chemistry or gravity—were established at the big bang? If not, when and how did they appear?

To know the origin of the universe is to understand the arising of a mental state.

To speak of the laws of nature or the rules of language implies a maker of laws and rules. The alternative is that laws develop as recurrent patterns.

Such regularities or recurrent patterns are like habits in behavior.

A law or rule is not applied to a state or process but is extracted from its uniformity.

The primary candidate for a mental law is qualitative partition. How would this appear in the micro-physical world? In fractals? In fission?

The rules of chess that are deduced from the movement of the pieces are assumed to guide the players. However, the game is driven by strategies that are constrained by the rules.

Reason

Feeling points the direction that reason wants to go

REASON IS NOT A guide to action but a justification of impulse. The question is whether consciousness initiates or blocks an act. If so, how does it work? If not, why did it evolve? Consciousness and the relation to brain are taken to be the most complex problems in theory of mind, but consciousness is not a fixed thing. It is a trajectory that goes from the core of mind to its external surface, more vivid with imagery in the context of perception. As a relation, what does consciousness have to do with love or any feeling other than as acknowledgement?

Before the self appears, there is a distinction of subjective and objective, and an awareness of the outer, not the inner

With the partition of the self, consciousness is obligatory

A self creates what it apprehends; acts, objects, images, thoughts. This is all there is to being conscious, even in dream.

> Impersonal facts are useless.
> The brain is not a storehouse,
> It is a theme that parses irrelevancy.

Consciousness is necessary to the inadequacy of the automatic
Reason built on instinct has hunger as foundation
Success is to surpass one's limitations.
Happiness is to live within them.
Artifice not grounded in the organic is a stain on authenticity
Will rides the coattails of uncertainty as possibility becomes definite
What is true can only be demonstrated after it is decided
Some animals show grief on the death of an infant. Is this genuine mourning, or is it like a child that sulks over a lost toy?

Directional feeling gives subjective aim to outcomes we accept as intentional

The passage from self to thought is the trajectory of the intentional

The automatic precedes the volitional, but deliberation prepares the way for spontaneity

Education

*If mind develops from generality to specificity,
should education follow the same pattern?*

APART FROM THE RUNNING debate over whether the aim of education should be inculcation or creative individuality—a great books course or a tribute to diversity—there are few definitive studies on the outcomes of either goal, and fewer still on the methods to achieve them. On the other hand, there is little doubt that the intelligent usually do better in life, at least from the standpoint of achievement if not happiness. Is this because they are smarter or better educated, seek more education, are more likely to be admitted to a good school, or do employers seek and pay more for those with a college degree? The first question is how important is a formal education in college, and what sort of education should it be, apart from the influences of others and the contacts that it breeds? College graduates make more money, but what part of this is a result of learning or having a degree? I am not referring to an advanced degree or specialized training in a profession such as law or science, where dedication and proficiency in one line of study are essential.

It strikes me that most college graduates are still uneducated, and those who are have acquired knowledge largely on their own or by exposure to others. Most college graduates have read few good books that are not mandatory, know little of fine music unless exposed outside, are ignorant of mathematics beyond a simple level, and show more interest in getting a job than furthering their education. The long-standing debate continues as to a generalized or specialized education, though there is little evidence a generalized education produces more than useless dilettantes, or that a specialized education leads to uncultured nerds, though the latter is preparation for a career, a profession or a trade.

Education

Kant taught for the mediocre, since the imbeciles were beyond help and the geniuses would help themselves. Some have wondered if education is harmful, a system of imprisonment to spare parents the nuisance of their children, that is, a sheltered workshop or day care for young adults. Others such as Dewey thought education should emphasize progressive values and adapt to individual needs. Is the purpose of an education to fill empty "bins" in the brain with information, prepare one for life and work, instill values, produce individuals who can participate in social and political activities, find one's self, teach critical thinking and creativity (if possible), promote curiosity, all of the above or something else entirely?

A strong case can be made for a targeted education in a variety of areas, but what is the value of a general education? In most people, vocabulary grows little after early adolescence, tastes and inclinations are often established relatively early in life, unusual talents are apparent, sports and fitness training have little to do with academics, grades matter only for further education and celebrated drop-outs in various fields betray the formulaic belief that college=success. Considering the expense of college, the prolongation of adolescence and dependency, the delay in starting a career, the difficulty finding a job, the mere vanity of a degree, the question demands a serious answer.

My own view is that once the basics are learned, education should focus on conceptual growth; that is, increasing the range and diversity of existing concepts, or enlarging them to incorporate novel ingredients. In a word, begin with what the student knows and build on that. Though there is relative uniformity of concepts in a given society, this implies an approach tailored to the individual. There should be an attempt to decipher a person's conceptual life, allowing knowledge to blossom organically through a kind of parasitic infestation. Whether this involves woodworking or creative writing, a method to augment conceptual growth could depend on presenting material not only directly but in the periphery of awareness; a mode of learning that is incidental or adventitious to the particularities of instruction.

There should be a shift from the obvious to the implicit, from data to context, from fact to value. Perhaps there should be exercises in analogy and metaphoric thinking. Ten minutes of enforced silence or meditation to stimulate inner thought and imagination might accomplish more than is imparted in an hour. The center of fixed attention should be selected not only for the information to be conveyed, but for the impact of the contextual background. Problem-solving should be displaced from external games and scores to introspective analysis. Object-relations should be stoked in terms of predecessors in the imagination. Instead of knowledge that entails rote learning, projects should require research and the formation of novel concepts independent of spoon-fed data. The goal is for students to avoid a passive ingestion of useless, irrelevant or rapidly forgotten data, and to resist the propaganda or deranged attitudes of their teachers in order to engage in spirited independent thought.

From the standpoint of the teacher, lively and informed confrontation is preferable to mute consensus or indulgence. The instructor should at least attempt to promulgate novel ideation, especially an informed challenge to conventional thought. For many professors who teach the same course year after year, the lectures are much the same though the faces change. Now and then the textbooks are updated, but there is a tendency to lapse into the familiar (like the behaviorist who said he could sleep during his lecture and deliver it by stimulus-response chains). Teachers have to be receptive to novelty, to a deviation from the norm, to the tangential, to attempts to go beyond the formulaic. As an example of an inspired teacher, Whitehead gave Gertrude Stein an A on a philosophy final even though she wrote that it was too beautiful a day to spend taking an examination. He found the logic impeccable.

ભ

We probably lose a trillion synapses by the age of 12, more by 18. How should this influence the goals of education?

The carnival of presentations from one lecture hall to the next is the academic equivalent of the snake oil salesman taking his wagon to neighboring towns. There is a sleazy aspect to self-serving propaganda but what else is one to do?

Parcellation explains why generality is at risk and capacity is lost by learning what we know.

If learning decreases connectivity and/or redundancy in the brain, what should we make of this phenomenon?

The question is how to exploit the possibilities in the generality of connectivity before specification closes it down.

Conscious information is psychically inert. Only in recollection—incomplete revival—does the material come into play.

We do not put coals on the top floor when the furnace is in the basement.

Education

What we know is important for skill, but concepts flourish prior to the acquisition of skill or when spontaneity is retarded

I was surprised how the work I read in my teens, such as Bergson and Cassirer, recurred, unaware, in my writing 40 years later.

Mentoring passes on knowledge not found in the books. Without it, the simpleton in any field is immediately exposed.

Education gives the tools but cannot tell you how to use them.

Students want the pearls; my interest is the oyster, which is where the pearls come from.

Why in spite of great universities do we live in an age of mediocrity?

Has innovation in technology replaced genius in creativity?

Borges wrote of a man with total recall but a complete lack of concepts. We do not build concepts from data. The concepts come first.

Typically, the memory savant has difficulties with productive thinking.

What is enormous learning if it does not grow organically? We all know people with immense learning who seem incapable of original thought.

Hans Reichenbach warned that historical study in physics might inhibit creative errors

Oliver Goldsmith wrote,

> "And still they gazed, and still the wonder grew,
> That one small head could carry all he knew".

No matter how much you learn, your brain will not have the accessible capacity of a cell phone. This is surprising in view of the trillions of cells and connections, but it shows that the function of the brain is not to store information but to generate it.

One can transfer information, but how does one teach insight?

I can't help but think that the greatest motivation is often pleasing a parent.

Ideally, the student who completes high school should have had the equivalent of a college education. This is the case with most European schools.

Why don't we teach, *inter alia*, languages in the first grade before the critical period shuts down?

Like flowers that turn to the sun, the ordinary cluster on the mean.

It is said that about 90% of people think they have above-average intelligence. Are half of them idiots, or are we missing something?

My brother, a professor of sociology at the University of Maryland, was criticized for teaching at a Harvard level. Should a professor adapt his teaching to accommodate the dullards?

But of course, even the Buddha had three discourses.

Not a natural teacher, I am unable to collaborate with students without a common baseline, reluctant to pass on systematically a mass of dead knowledge and critiqued for an off-the-cuff style.

Ironic that the most influential American scholar of the second half of the 20th century, Noam Chomsky, will likely be remembered, if at all, more for his influence and polemics than his linguistics and political science. A gracious man, unlike the rabidity of his most adept students, he prevailed in debate by inundating his adversary with data.

Blinded by the light of a great man, many are resigned to commentary on his writings, failing to explore what might have been left unwritten.

Is it sensible to structure education to turn out original thinkers? There are so few of them.

Many of the most intelligent spend a lifetime contesting a small part of a great thinker's work. Is this a useful activity?

I believe a deep knowledge of William James is enough to become reasonably proficient in philosophical psychology, as with Freud in psychoanalysis.

If someone achieves fame after they are dead, it may be because the contemporary generation of critics has also died and the work can have a fresh reading.

The Italians have a saying that the child who is too good is good for nothing. Here, we medicate those with high spirit.

It is perhaps an unpleasant truth that learning disability is a medical term for a stupid child.

A parent is dismayed when a child falls short of their expectations, but once it is realized that the child's capacity is limited, happiness not accomplishment should be the goal.

The funding for remediation of the intractable would be better spent on children who are gifted. Tutor the exceptional, not the retarded.

My library

Pity my library is on the shelves and not in my head.

THE FEW THOUSAND DUSTY volumes that overflow the shelves of my apartment are my imaginary companions in the day and my silent bedmates at night. A comfort by their presence, they are an inspiration by the lifetimes devoted to their composition, precious in their rarity. Equally a history of my field of study and a chronicle of the progression of my own thought, a scholarly adventure at home that travels from recondite topics to the philosophical generalities in which they are nested, surrounded by centuries of experience and study, ideas floating in the air, the dedication, the historical tide, those who swim in the flow and those who labor on the banks, colleagues, friends, antagonists, lives bypassed and wasted, pages watermarked, uncut, volumes brilliant but rarely cited, tomes by scholars like Henri Ey and Hartwig Kuhlenbeck who passed unnoticed, paths untraveled by others, waking from oblivion, coming to life in my armchair, refreshed, bathed in my imagination, each with its neighbor in spirited conversation.

When I was young, before Google transformed libraries into deserts, before book dealers disappeared into the internet, browsing in used bookstores in hopes of discovering inexpensive jewels hidden in the stacks, was for me an expedition to a distant land that uncovered a rare artifact or ancient tomb. There were times, I confess, when finding an old volume in a university library that had never been checked out— never held in the eager hands of an appreciative reader—compelled me to adopt the treasure. I removed it to a loving foster home, rescued from incarceration without visitation, with the mellow satisfaction on learning that one of my own books had been borrowed and never returned, I do not say stolen for it was an act of love. A tattered thesis, a first edition hardcover, a searched-for work on some esoteric theme retrieved from obscurity and indifference to spend its days in warm fellowship with like-minded companions all similarly absorbed in study and ideas.

Adrift in books no less real and palpable than the actual world, the dank smell of aging volumes in the shaded chambers of my cramped apartment are sweeter than Spring flowers on a sunlit day. This is not a life of monkish seclusion in a literary mausoleum but a retreat to a world of thought from the fatigue of daily life, obligations, responsibilities. Sated by all kinds of pleasures, the inexhaustibility of nature and the varieties of social interaction, the warmth of family, travel, old and new friendships, students, lectures—all of which were a joy—but also the cultish obsession with the nature of mind and brain, enticed me to the quiet sanctity of this cemeterial ground. When I consider the value of the material in the books—especially those works of a bygone century that were most compatible with my thought—or when I reminisce on the fascination with neurological disorders, the prancing ambitions at seminars, the mock show of interest, the conversations with colleagues who tried to convince me of the importance of their own petty work, it was never the actual data, which were dutifully absorbed, as the stimulus to ideas well beyond the mainstream that leapt from the books and discourse like startled gazelles.

∽

Much that is forgotten is what passes for discovery. Most discovery is re-discovery with a different method.

I once asked a learned friend to cite an experiment in 50 years of psychology that was decisive. He could only think of a paper on statistics. The point is, in psychology, every experiment has many deficiencies and every result has different conclusions. This implies that psychology is not a science in spite of attempts to put it on a quantitative basis.

Still alive, I watch my own work pass into history, perhaps to come alive again at another time in another library.

Some books, like Sartre's *Being and Nothingness*, or Heidegger's *Being and Time*, or Soury's two volume *Système Nerveux Central*, or my set of Charles Peirce, I've saved to read for a long ocean voyage that will surely never take place. If my brain was truly a computer, I would scan them into files. But would I profit from the storage?

When she was angry, she threatened to burn my library. Women have an uncanny knack for a man's Achilles heel

My library

Freud's library in New York was pilfered and desecrated, with the initial signed page torn off. Sadly, the celebrity of the writer counted more than the content of the works

I hold no special attachment to my signed copies of Whitehead, but the feel of a first edition makes reading more enjoyable.

The eventual parting with my library is painful though I read very little these days.

As a form of revenge on a mistress, the widow of a well-known philosopher offered a dealer a substantial sum to cart away his library—the enemy of the marriage—a case of jealousy by neglect.

We all need diversion. If the eyes cannot move, we cannot see.

Phrenology

Is mind localized in brain, or is brain localized in mind?

PHRENOLOGY IS THE STUDY of functions in the brain by bumps on the skull, dating back to 1805, to the earliest work by Gall who attempted to localize faculties in the brain at a time when the brain appeared to function as a whole. The shift from generality to locality of representation continued with his student, Bouillaud, a neurologist and head of the French phrenology society, whose study in 1825 of speech loss in over 100 cases of frontal lobe damage seemed to confirm his teacher's supposition. This led to Paul Broca, a student of Bouillaud, whose famous 1861 paper with necropsy in a frontal speech case initiated scientific study of brain localization. The sequence from Gall to Broca is also a classic instance of the rise of materialism, with a progression from philosophical speculation to clinical description to anatomical demonstration. Broca, actually the last of the phrenologists, is now, ironically, regarded as the father of the brain science of language. Parenthetically, phrenology is an illustration of how a correlation—language and the frontal lobe—may accidentally be correct even if its rationale is defective. Later studies would relate language primarily to the left hemisphere, define phonological and grammatical deficits more precisely, and pin down regions of the frontal lobe with greater accuracy, even correlating some aspects of grammar and its defects with the genome.

While the relation of regional brain size to the skull is uncertain—even in the fossil record (endocasts)—the phrenological idea persists in the faculty psychology of cognitive science. The notion that cerebral dominance is due to a larger left brain is consistent with this doctrine. It was pointed out long ago that the brain volume of a gorilla is comparable to that of some African bushmen, or dwarfs who are capable of behavior, including language, superior to apes. On the other hand, man and ape cannot be

Phrenology

differentiated by microscopic examination of a piece of cortical tissue, so it is not size alone or (probably) fine structure, but process and specification that are critical.

∽

A fertile mistake is preferable to a barren proof.

Scientific advance often comes of error or as a byproduct of looking for something else if the scientist has an open mind.

Is Gall's localization of amativeness or destructiveness in the brain so different from modern researchers who localize love or a moral sense from brain imaging?

The question is not only what is localized—functions, faculties, representations, skills, strategies, operations and so on—but what is meant by localization, and how and where is anything localized.

How would one localize a category, or its members, which are also categories?

Localization depends on spatial thinking, but mentality is temporal. The phrenology concept that began 200 years ago on an erroneous basis has continued to the present.

Probably it is the nature of thought that limits how we think. This would explain why such muddled thinking persists in spite of its obvious deficiencies.

To localize the word "chair" is not to point to an area but to identify all the phases through which the word is derived.

Localize a faculty and you avoid having to account for its contents.

The crudest way to get around the problem—mind and brain, spirit and matter, god and the physical world—is to retain the physical and dispense with the mental, a not so serious philosophy that is termed eliminativism.

Can we say the mind that denies the mental does not exist? If we say the physical brain, not the mind, denies the mental, how could the brain deny a mentality of which it is not aware?

If mind is replaced by brain, with which it is identical, how can brain elaborate mind if brain is physical process? There is a self-referential paradox here not unlike that of the Cretan liar (Epimenides).

We have direct or immediate experience of mind, while the physical is a product of inference.

For most, a thought unfolds in many sentences. For me, each sentence is a thought.

Reflections on Mind and the Image of Reality

On brain imaging, the same area is active on moving an arm, attempting to move a phantom limb in an amputee and imagining a movement. However, passive movement does not, I believe, activate the area, although a monkey watching a limb movement in another animal may elicit mirror activation. Electrical stimulation of the area may produce limb movement that feels passive. Similarly, a memory may be evoked on repeated stimulation of areas in the temporal lobe but excision of the area does not abolish the memory. So what exactly is localized?

I have often thought that the relation of mind and brain is a problem that will never be solved.

PART V

Concluding Thoughts

Concentration and Meditation

Does concentration on nothing lead to thought or vacuity?

MY MANTRA IS FROM a well-known sutra that goes: gate gate pāragate pārasaṃgate bodhi svāhā, which means—though meaning is not important to a mantra—gone, gone, far gone, gone beyond, enlightenment! It alludes to a higher state of consciousness, the transition from life to death, but it also reminds us of the common experience in India of taking a ferry boat to an unseen shore through mist and haze. Perhaps the goal of eliminating concepts or thoughts or feelings so the emptied mind can be a receptacle for wisdom or transcendence is a way to achieve the ineffable. But speaking for myself, it is not possible, as one with childhood ADHD, to concentrate on a repetitious phrase for more than a few minutes. Yet, I can be lost in thought, oblivious to my surroundings, and realize a depth of focal concentration for hours. I suppose the mantra is an aid to those unable to concentrate or avoid distraction, or with nothing to concentrate on. The practice—from one who occasionally dives into very deep waters—seems a method designed to remove distraction in the hope for personal revelation.

This type of meditation differs from the inwardly-inspired retreat of nature or religious mystics, who seek oneness with god or the absolute. Ordinary meditation aims to free the mind from other preoccupations in the expectation that an extraordinary insight may occur. Perhaps it does, but more often the experience is one of relaxation and liberation from the here and now. Then, of course, apart from the intuitions that give original ideas, where the focus of concentration is or has been on a particular problem, there is the question of what constitutes enlightenment, what is experienced in meditation that is not experienced in ordinary thought, what great insight is waiting?

Reflections on Mind and the Image of Reality

Probably, enlightenment gives intensity and conviction to ideas that were formerly entertained. The intensity is the unwavering focus on an idea that, before meditation, was one idea among many. In this respect, the enlightenment of the Buddha, the Noble Eightfold path, seems trivial.

> The navel was the primal aim
> But after that, nothing came
> Yet meditation found a home
> When he called his phallus Om.

> Think on empty space and space stays empty.
> Think on a tree and history unfolds.

The Kumbh Mela! A congregation in Varanasi every 13 years—a bar mitzvah for holy men—half-way yogas who lecture in tents, eccentrics with special devotions, some sleep naked on crematory ash, the standing bubbas with elephantine legs. One pulled a car with his dick. Is this truly the path to nirvana?

I see no difference in the emptiness of pure relations and complete annihilation.

The question is what the young are seeking and why. There is no genuine self. Enlightenment takes years of thought and study, and even then, amounts to what?

How do you have cravings without a craver (Danto)? Desires don't occur in a vacuum.

The feeling of oneness with god's love is one form of (delusional) enlightenment. What are the others?

To think the world is illusion is one thing, to feel it another.

Does the content or nature of enlightenment differ from one person to another or is there one insight common to all?

On falling asleep

After hours of sleep or anesthesia, I awake and am still myself.
How do we explain the return of the self after hours of non-self?

Is LIFE A DREAM? The two arguments against the possibility are the coherence of wakefulness and the faith that god is not a deceiver. Perhaps god is a deceiver. We are deceived in so many other ways; in the substantiality of objects, the reality of time, the meaningfulness of life. Leibniz wrote that the true criterion we are not dreaming is the connectedness of waking phenomena. But the feeling of reality does not appeal to a criterion. Are coherent dreams judged more real, than a waking experience? I doubt it. Coherence in perception owes to the temporal order achieved out of the simultaneity of dream. I dreamt a memory of the past. I remember a dream of the present. Which is more real? The man who dreamt he was a butterfly in Zhuangzi's dream was not a man dreaming but an imaginary butterfly, as is the man waking in the butterfly's dream. The dream is as real as anything else. When a dream is recognized as unreal or as a memory, and so falsified, the past in the dream is part of the consciousness of waking. A dream is a memory displaced to a past that wakefulness creates.

I have tried many times to retain an awareness of falling asleep but, except for anesthesia, in which it is possible to be aware of the precise instant of becoming unconscious, there is always an amnesia for the transition. For many years, in a kind of transitional state, with my eyes open and attention passive to the field, I had frequent hypnagogic hallucinations, silent, agonized, colorful faces contorted beyond description, more vivid than in life. Any attempt to look directly at the face, even an effort to avoid looking, resulted in its disappearance. This involuntary phase occurred in the transition to sleep, perhaps to dream, but still the exact moment of sleep eluded me. Loss of vision, due to occipital damage, passes through a hallucinatory stage resulting in a lack of transition to dreamless sleep. Is hypnagogia a part of this phenomenon? The lack of memory for falling asleep resembles the brief retrograde amnesia common with concussions. Similarly, on waking, I often do not recall precisely what I was discussing or reading just prior to sleep.

The intentionality of waking consciousness decomposes to intermediate phases that, in the relation of self to object, include hypnagogic imagery, transitional states, auto-symbolic imagery and dream. Lucid dreaming resembles the hypnagogic state in that the self is conscious of private content. In hallucinatory or dream-like states, attention concentrates in a face or scenic image. As a heightened awareness of external objects occurs in some people, phases of reduced intensity occur in fatigue and intoxication. But the change is not like a dimmer on a light switch for each gradation is qualitatively different. A critical shift is a diminished focal attention without vividness of feeling for widespread detail. This resembles the inattention to the external but without greater inwardness.

Among the features of dreams that hold great interest in Asian thought, fables and myth, are the transformations of shape and person and the attenuation of subjective time. The mutation of objects, the change from one person to another, the fusion of memory and perceptual immediacy, or the commingling of the present with the historical, bring to life the concurrence of past and present in a single image, a fusion of an individual and events widely separated in space and time. In the fleeting present of the dream, memories lose their pastness such that the distant past assumes a present reality. In the dream world, the present is all there is; past and future never develop. The attempt to recapture the past in present consciousness through meditative states grows out of the non-temporality of the dream, and the fragility and recurrence of subjective time in the passage of pure succession.

At Einstein's suggestion, Piaget found that space and time were bound together in young children. For example, going faster takes more time for the younger children, while in older children, space and time are perceived separately. In brain damage, time and space are mediated by separate systems: time is altered with disorders of memory; space breaks down as an impairment of object-relations. Einstein supposed his "child-like" concept of space-time owed to his slow development. In dream, the succession of spatial images is compressed in a simultaneity that, on waking, unfolds into serial order, implying a commonalty of space and time. Dream space is curved; it is palpable, not empty. The demonstration of gravitational waves shows that space, like dream, is not empty but has a "fabric". The outward expansion of the universe and the progression from a singularity to a multiplicity are analogous to the iterated development of objects from core unity to surface multiplicity. Add this to the anthropic principle, an event ontology and the observer effect in micro-physics, and the conclusion is inescapable that the properties and laws of mind are identical to those of physics.

∾

In dream, the absence of pastness and futurity leave a durationless present in which events apprehended on waking recover the temporal order compressed in simultaneity.

Is the brief memory of most dreams on waking part of the unconscious fabric of experience? If so, what happens to unrecollected dreams?

We recall a memory and we recall having the experience of reminiscence. These are different states. But is lack of recall of dreams because it would be a memory of a memory?

Jung built his theory on his dreams, or did his theory determine the kind of dreams he had?

Synchronicity is possible in the simultaneity of a mass dream. It would also be possible if we were dreams in god's mind. Over millions of years, the sleeping Brahma dreams a world, then he wakes briefly to fall asleep again and dream another.

I wonder what happens between moments or mental states. Are there other worlds in the interstices of my own?

Is death an awakening from the dream of life (Fechner)? Or does the fantasy of a state beyond consciousness develop out of dream?

The noosphere is not a supra-conscious field but an absolute beneath the first spark of awareness.

The higher forms of consciousness in yogic practice are earlier forms of awareness to which consciousness descends.

The beauty of my garden disappears in the word and returns when thought is suspended.

To analyze beauty or love is like counting grains of sand as they slip through your fingers.

Are we the larval form of future humanity or the debris of a wondrous past?

Knowing begins when you recall and do not know whether dream or remembrance.

Were long past memories to become truly alive, they would be happening now!

The past in the present is necessary for conscious existence. Were the present in the past, we would disappear.

For this to occur is a time reversal, with the person vanishing into the past—not the actual past but the past of memory—while everyone else is vanishing into the future.

I suppose if I slept for 20 years I would be astonished at the physical change on waking but would my self be altered?

We can compare a mirror reflection against a memory, or a photo with a reflection, but what do we compare with the self? There is no image, and the memory of a former self is vague. Perhaps this is why in spite of old age, many still feel young.

The question arises in cases of severe amnesia, who may recall nothing over years but show maturation and personality development.

The examined life

The search for purpose can only begin when the hunger for experience is sated by the feast of life.

THE ART OF LIFE is to discover that which gives meaning to one's own life, and to pursue that discovery with passion to the limits of the possible. The goal of thought is to discover—if discoverable—the impersonal meaning or purpose that guides an individual life and explains the existence of human mind and organic form.

When Socrates dismissed the unexamined life as not worth living he was not referring to self-exploration of neurotic impulse but to serious thought on the nature, meaning and purpose of life, a goal that for many degrades to a psychic massage and a quest for personal understanding, through therapy, illumination or meditative trance, a short-cut for sustained thought and a panacea for individuality and social belonging, none of which bear on the Socratic admonition. The genesis of perfunctory insight or self-analysis is dilettantism, a collapse of wisdom to gullibility, of genuine knowledge to specious acquaintance, of struggle to cleansing.

What could be the purpose of life beyond endless propagation? The gift of inquiry? Creative thought? For the absolute idealist, or those of anthropic persuasion, human mind is essential to the laws of the universe, such that the process of thought not only depends on but creates the laws of physics which the universe displays or, perhaps less implausibly, a deeper monism in relation to which mind and world are comprehensible. Those who look to the world for meaning will come up empty-handed. There is process and dynamic but no meaning to the rocks, craters and gases of inorganic matter other than continual reappearance. For human thought to evolve in concert with nature, consciousness generates meaning in a world that would otherwise be meaningless. This supposes an Aristotelian final cause toward which life is moving, with the goal of importing meaning into the universe which, were there to be purpose in the forward direction or teleology of evolutionary nature, would be the mind and purpose of god.

The consolation of uncovering patterns or regularities in mind/brain process that correlate with the process of change in nature gives meaning to human consciousness. This is not the meaning of an individual life, but recognition of and participation in the uniformity of process. The concept of eternal recurrence in some cultures extends the aim of meaning or purpose to its abolition. The goal is to finally get off the périphérique, the cycle of return, but to what end? To escape suffering in a future life has little appeal to the contented or for that matter to the rational. Recurrence is foundational to change, without which no entity or organism can exist. In Indian philosophy, release from samsara is an end to recurrence (existence), which implies that nirvana is not a state but an absence of a hellish afterlife.

For the average individual, meaning and purpose apply to conventions of family, success, comfort and healthy living, or to such reassuring tropes as leaving the world a better place or helping the less fortunate, worthwhile endeavors, but on a cosmic scale, the view from outside, with death an abiding companion, what is there to which meaning could possibly apply?

∽

For those who are aware, the void filled by work, travel and family grows to a solitary abyss.

Wit and humor are the protests of irreconcilables. This is especially so in generation and involution, growth and mortality.

The feeling of positive advance in life is the forward thrust of recurrence that carries the world into novelty.

If we cannot prepare for the contingencies of life, how can we prepare for the certainty of death?

The incompatibility of death with the surge to the future mitigates the conviction that life will ever end.

I believe the awareness of mortality is necessary for immortal works of art and thought. In the fragility and urgency of life, the creative is an illusory conquest of the stark reality of death

The pursuit of pleasure: a merciful respite from boredom and the futility of speculation.

Too much questioning, one falls in a pit.

The subjective aim in every act of thought transports the self into definiteness, but the potential from which the mental state arises recurs as possibilities inherent in actuality. The paradox is that mind devolves to the potential out of which it originates.

The objective past is immortal. It cannot be erased, unlike pleasures that leave no trace.

Look for meaning in death as well as in life.

Finally, can we say the purpose of life is to live with few regrets?

Psychoanalysis and the Family

Knowing that parents convey the genes of their parents is to wonder if trans-generational factors are more important than the parental endowment.

MERCIFULLY, I HAVE BEEN spared those unhappy deep-rooted events of childhood that comprise a handful of predictable scenarios in the traumatic history of the self-absorbed. This resulted in my interest in the universals of mind rather than the particulars of personality. Such variations in maturation, appearance, situation, luck and opportunity in life, the infinitude of looks, likes and dislikes, the fingerprints and genes of personality, are the stuff of novels, conversations and personal reflection, but no matter how spectacular the variations, an individual is an instance of just so many themes of family life. From the bird's eye view of the philosopher, happy and unhappy families, *pace* Tolstoy, owe to much the same conditions: drives, needs, jealousies and so on, that constitute the inventory of tensions, satisfactions, acts selfish or generous, work, leisure, provocations and irritations that fill the vacant hours through which life passes. In this perspective, the smiles and scars that shape individuality are of less interest to me than the categories they instantiate. A lack or excess of maternal love, disengagement, abuse, bonding, estrangement, confidence, aggrievements, are mere gossip compared to the origin and nature of love, disdain, maternal instinct, aggression, parenting.

For most, the intrigue is in the eccentricities, not the generalities behind them. To a psychoanalyst, certain themes recur in all individuals— oedipal, castration—to account for the inevitable traumas that are held to accompany childhood experience. The personal tragedy of life begins with birth, passes to alienation and the finality that awaits us all. Life is lived in concrete fact, not in abstraction, but an aptitude for the invariant has, for me, a deeper appeal than the particular. This is the case in all aspects of life, for example, the multiplicity of languages compared to the elusiveness of universals, but it is the discovery of universals, for example, the evolutionary diversity explained by natural selection, that is more satisfying than a focus on the occasions into which they distribute.

Perhaps this frame of mind is also a result of dealing with catastrophic illness in neurology. The result is impatience with the relative triviality of family dysfunction, the marks of its impact and obsession with its degree, and the extent to which it is exploited by professional healers of bruised psyches. One such friend, honest to a fault, an analyst who insisted he was not a shrink but a stretch, when asked the criteria for psychoanalysis said "healthy and rich"! The narcissism of psychotherapy is the primary symptom left untreated, though self-love and self-loathing are the motive force. The impious peddler who recommends a psychic emetic for everyone continues to unearth material to enrich the sources of unhappiness and justify perpetual treatment. Indeed, the psychoses, even though they are resistant to treatment and not occasioned by childhood distress, hold greater interest for theory of mind than the neuroses. Such diversity, like a Bosch triptych, dots the landscape of imagined and unimaginable forms.

My paternal grandparents came to New York in the late 1800's from Odessa. My grandfather was one of two in a family of 14 to survive the brutal winters and febrile illnesses in childhood. An opera loving communist and an intellectual who fomented revolution in a Danbury Stetson hat factory, he has my lasting affection for his legendary collection of Caruso LP's. My grandmother, a seamstress and older than he, was said by my mother to be sweet, orderly and a terrible nag. By all accounts an unloving couple, they died in their late 50's.

First there was the loss of Jacob, my namesake, when I was six months in mother's belly; then Rebecca, for whom my brother Richard was named a year later, scarcely to be mentioned again. In a faint echo of Keats, "Was it a vision, or a waking dream? Fled is that music. Do I wake or sleep", she whispered "ales a cholem" (all is a dream) as she died.

And so, my father, the oldest of three, was said to not visibly grieve the death of his father, burying his parents along with his hopes of giving them a better life. Not a religious man in the usual sense, he walked his father's empty shoes around the block to liberate his soul and, like the modern custom of paying orphans to perform Kaddish he returned to work and paid others to perform the services. Kingsley said the African mind

Reflections on Mind and the Image of Reality

approaches all things from a spiritual point of view. This is not faith, which is a suspension of reason, but an irrational element in the mind that invites the subjective into acts of signification. It is the heart of animism and the mystical sensitivity. Father's beliefs, and mine, were that god does not animate a passive nature with divine spirit; rather, the spirit in nature is god's presence in the universe. He did not ask, but:

> "What if all of animated nature
> Be but organic Harps diversely fram'd
> That tremble into thought, as o'er them sweeps
> Plastic and vast, an intellectual Breeze
> At once the soul of each, and god of all?"

There is no necessity for the "intellectual breeze" of which Coleridge wrote so beautifully. The harps of nature—superstring vibrations—seething with vitality as part of the intrinsic rhythm in its progression, in grandeur and immensity, are the animating force of the physical and organic world.

Father believed this to be so even if he could not have expressed it in careful language. He was not literary, but with his boyish candor, gentleness of heart, reverence for the life around him, awe and sensitivity, he could have been a Haiku poet on a pilgrimage about the countryside. He too could have written that "no joyless forms shall regulate our living calendar." We all know the false pretension of modesty but rarely do we encounter a genuine attitude of secular devotion, a simplicity and self-effacement before the revelation of god in all his aspects. As George Eliot wrote, the sunshine of far-off years lives in us and transforms our perceptions into love, and so it was that this kindly business man, without a grain of arrogance or spite, was for me inspirational as a reminder of the humility and consecration that nature requires of her votaries if, with a receptive heart, they are to be given mute instruction at the living throne of deity.

Father died in his sleep at 88 after years of debilitation and suffering. Three days after it left him, the breath of my father entered my body in a fit of shuddering on waking from a dream. I was dressed in white in a hospital bed as a phantom approached me, holding out her hand she offered herself to me, floated under my body, kissed me smiling and I said as I held her, "you know, I'm not really." and awoke in a chill with the word "sick" on my lips, pale as a ghost, sensing the soul of the father reborn in the son.

The Kabbalists speak of *gilgul,* the transmigration of souls. In the *bardo* of the Tibetans, the living and the newly dead are in contact. The

PSYCHOANALYSIS AND THE FAMILY

ungwulan of the *Aruntas* hovers near the camp after death observing those who remain. The primitives have their initiation rites by which the vital spirit is transferred from one corporeal frame to another. Frazer mentions a Basque legend of the hunter who said he was killed by a bear, which then breathed its soul into him, so that now he was animated by the bear's soul. For me, the myth of the bear, the motion of the spirit, the timelessness of dream are the soul of eternity, the time that hovers on the passage of moments like a rainbow in the sunshine. So my father, little did I know the past would not die with you, that I, your soul, would cease to live as your son but that we, from that moment, would be a single form in change.

Although my mother was a blessing to her sons, charismatic with sparkling, cynical wit, our daily guide and confessor, it is my father, in the tacit understanding that passes between men, or father and son, that I owe my mystical bias, reverence for nature, search for general laws, principles or universals, the glacial pace of my thought process, my social discomfort, and the shift from clinic to theory and back, or from academia to business.

∼

As the rings of an oak record the seasons, a family and its heartaches are etched into the grains of personality.

Can one predict outcomes from childhood? One child suffers, another profits, from lavish mothering; the same for maternal neglect.

What kind of theory explains opposite outcomes from similar conditions, and similar outcomes from opposite conditions?

Why do siblings differ as much among themselves as with those of a neighbor?

A child is dissatisfied with who they are if there is discord with the inner parent.

Deeper than the lyrics of women are the songs without words of men.

Women bond in chatter, men in silence; women in feeling, men in doing.

I would suppose, according to their influence, presidents who initiate a war had strong fathers; those who maintain the peace were raised by mothers, the one paternalistic, masculine, the other co-dependent.

Endowment

What would you prefer, my dear, a comfortable life and inheritance with a decent man or a life of excitement and torment that ends in penury?

ON MY 70TH BIRTHDAY, it was a shock to suddenly realize I was old. This left me with a choice, to struggle against aging with diet and exercise, or to acquiesce to the natural course of things and settle into approaching decrepitude. The first option required a sustained commitment to indigestible meals and daily workouts with no assurance that fighting the inevitable will postpone it, nor that any benefit would offset the time and energy expended. The latter option had greater appeal so long as it did not guarantee a hastier exit. On the contrary, the conservation of strength and enjoyment of sustenance would surely contribute to what pleasures could be gleaned in my declining years. The best course of action was to live at a comfortable pace, take pleasures as they come, continue writing even if the work is never published, since it gives satisfaction and helps to fill my days, and make an effort to organize my affairs for my darling younger wife, Carine, my three fine sons and one female spawn of Lear. My boys each have a different mother to highlight the paternal endowment, even if my frequent absence spared them much exposure. They are all tall, handsome, intelligent, with confidence, ambition, and tenderness, and interests ranging from art and politics to business.

A sense of responsibility instilled in childhood can cause genuine love to be replaced by duty or obligation. In our village in the south of France lives an elderly American woman left, as they say, without a sous. She sleeps in winter in a small unheated house beneath four collies for warmth, toothless and alone, but spins marvelous tales of adventures with famous writers and artists in the 50's: "Norman Mailer was not so macho in the bed; Robert Lowell, now, that was a man". She was widowed by a brilliant, erratic, alcoholic, little-known and largely unpublished Irish poet of the same artistic circle who carried on adulteries at home, spent her considerable fortune, insulted everyone, berated her and left her penniless Yet in spite of it all, and after dozens of affairs with men of talent, he was, she proclaimed, the great love of her life, an inheritance more precious than gold, regardless of whether she lived with him or through him. She recounted all this at our home in spirited and engaging conversation with Erika Jong who, perhaps no less profligate when young and beautiful, seemed to have a strong literary interest in her story.

And so, what would you prefer my dear, a comfortable life or a life of excitement and torment that ends in penury? Certainly, if your love is so strong there is hardly a choice. You might as well give all to him and commit suicide when it ends. Passion fades or is kept alive by suffering. Agitation in an unruly romance is the fuel of what passes for wild love and sacrifice, a surrogate passion to make you feel vividly alive. If you choose a safer path, the reward may be independence and autonomy, which are only threatened by the lure of passion and a fall from the knolls onto the rocks. Would you relinquish all for the memory of a great love—or a love that seems great in retrospect—or would you live, loveless, for a future of comfort and ease? Is memory a grotto of safety from the heartache of the present, or does the future only beckon the courageous?

༒

A narrow escape is an adventure. A harrowing occasion is an experience. The memory of the past tends to favor pleasure over pain. Is this why, in memory, love triumphs over suffering?

It is a quirk of memory that events tend to be recalled in a more positive light. The feeling is not revived as vividly as the event.

The romantic who takes a moment of passion for a lifetime of sorrow cherishes the memory to justify the choice.

In that duty subordinates will, it is a restraint on self-interest, but like habit, it can suffocate desire.

Where else but in the military is honor found in abundance? It loses meaning in a culture of indulgence.

Looking back and regret

Subjective time imitates but does not replicate physical time.
The now of consciousness arises in the chinks of passage.

WHEN TOWARD THE END, one looks back and sees *en bloc* the entire course of a life and the choices leading up to the present, the pattern seems a fulfillment of a plan or destiny, as if the reel of a life unfolds like music from a score. The life-paths of friends and acquaintances over this span, though seen from a distance, also have the same quality with rare surprises. Looking to the future, options abound, but how unpredictable are decisions? If one were to deliberately act in an illogical or self-defeating way, or to act against character and self-interest, could this be interpreted as a mark of freedom, or would it still be an irresistible act? What would it take for an act to be genuinely free? Even a deliberate act in defiance of causal closure can be construed as determined by character, willfulness and so on.

A future that is open from the outlook of the present contrasts with the inevitability of acts from a retrospective point of view. This gives a tension between freedom and causation. The past seems a causal chain; the future is filled with possibility. Even if we cannot know the contingencies, opportunities, those taken and those lost, the response to change seems, in hindsight, fairly predictable. The temptation to imagine life in reverse brings into play stillborn acts and restraints that might otherwise have led to more desirable outcomes, but an honest judgment that takes into account naiveté, attitude, knowledge, experience and susceptibility to the influence of others at the time of the action should lead the individual to admit that a replay would likely be the same. When we regret earlier choices we do so from the standpoint of greater experience and maturity.

Is a life to be lived fully and open to happenstance and the unforeseen, or guided by a plan, a goal, a pre-determined path that is followed? The hippie and the tax attorney, the urge to follow one's bliss, as Joseph Campbell put it, or to hitch your wagon to a star, as Robert Browning advised. What is preferable, a life spent or misspent, living for the day or the future, seeking pleasure and leisure or narrow success, lifestyle or accomplishment, writing the score or listening to the music, generosity or miserliness, hoarding or sharing, agent or spectator, a life of action or a life of thought, commitment or acquiescence? The "what if" is a common if unanswerable question; what if I had pursued one path or the other, not lost a parent at an early age, stepped off the curb a second later, married this one not that, controlled my temper? On and on.

When it comes to choice, the more difficult the decision and the greater the parity of options, the more we are likely to regret. A course of action relatively uncontested implies greater self-realization no matter the outcome, and less justification for a what-if. Yet very often we come across an inflection point in life: to stay the course or drop out of school; to choose learning as a volunteer or take an ordinary job; to act or to hesitate. Such moments may be decisive steps on a path of no return. For some, like me, choice is instinctive, a natural inclination in one direction without self-doubt. For others, choice is so agonizing that whatever decision is made leaves a residue of uncertainty. The choice is not "whole-hearted"; it does not reflect the genuine aspirations of the person. I did not have a plan; rather, a tendency in one direction. Indeed, if there was a plan, I felt less an instigator than an instrument of its realization.

In my case, apart from an aversion to risky ventures, there were few conscious choices that followed deliberation, but rather, an instinctive gravitation in a direction that was felt to be natural and comfortable. My dictum was, if you have to think very long about what to do, unless it is obligatory, your heart is not in it and you should do nothing or something else. This applies primarily to those with the luxury of choice, not the mass of people doomed to a life of unremitting labor, exploitation and servitude, such that the choice is to work or to starve.

A critical decision occurred when I was drafted in 1967 at the height of the Vietnam War to which I was strongly opposed. The only rational option was to move to Canada, which I seriously considered, personally and with friends. Finally, it was not reason that motivated the decision but the feeling that I would never know whether the choice was based on reason or cowardice—to die as a soldier or live as a coward. So, as in most decisions, it boiled down to an emotional push—by fear—that decided the issue. And so, I was off to war.

Looking back also raises the question of why time passes so quickly as one ages? Is it because each day is a progressively smaller fraction of experience, or because the variety of experiences that fill duration in youth gives way to relative inactivity and routine later in life such that, in recollection, duration contracts for lack of novelty to expand it. Perhaps the rate of time passing is felt in relation to the expanse of the future. When aging seems far off in the future, time seems to be a commodity that can be spent or wasted with little cost. In youth, life seems to go on forever—as in a lover's promise—though there may be a greater sense of evanescence in young people with terminal illness.

Is the rate of time passing related to memory? In brain damage, time is affected by memory disorders, not spatial ones as space-time theory might predict. In cases of amnesia, two months may feel like two weeks. Presumably, there is a lack of recollection for events that punctuate and so reconstruct the duration of past time. Is the feeling of duration related to expectancy? For a young man anxious for a weekend date, the wait feels like an eternity, while for the elderly with little to look forward to, weekends come and go in a flash. If the episodic sequence of past events, like a melody, unfolds from a simultaneous representation, the greater the diversity within the simultaneity the more expansive will be the felt duration as events take on serial order. Perhaps in aging, the monotony of daily life accounts for the collapse of past time to an instant. The contrast is evident even in advanced years, when the sense of an open and endless time—looking back and looking ahead—is still not reconciled with the conviction of a foreshortened future.

∾

She went on loving after her lover died. How does one love a memory?

I felt the absence of my brother who died at 63, but now, closer to my own death, his absence has become a presence as I feel him beside me.

The test of true love is to continue loving after the beloved is gone. Some say it is important to "move on," and resilient people do, but the past will always be the present for a great loss.

The unsung song of my life has few scherzos, no crescendos and an unwritten coda

When I describe a happy childhood, my psychoanalyst friends think I must be in denial, a handy mechanism for those who disagree

The future does not exist, yet we all live for it.

Looking back and regret

To live in or for the future is not possible, since it constantly becomes the past, passing through the present in the blink of an eye.

The artifice of a photograph is that a frozen moment is not the present of life. Nothing exists for an instant, though an artistic portrait conveys the person behind the smile.

A photograph revives a memory but the continuity with the image is felt in the memory, not the photograph.

If the past no longer exists and the future does not yet exist, existence is predicated on the present which, as an illusion, also does not exist as commonly supposed. What then is the relation of time to existence?

If things are in constant flux, at what point can we say something exists?

Not knowing what will happen in the next minute makes me feel that anything is possible.

There is no present outside of mind. The oncoming face of a block universe moves from before to after, not from present to future.

I believe a successful life, that is, one of good works, accomplishment and personal satisfaction, comes to those who find opportunity even in the most disheartening situations.

A placebo for regret is a forward-looking gaze

What is fate but causal certainty? If free will is the feeling of a self that decides, and if feeling, not reason, takes the person in some direction, inner-driven acts are like mild compulsions; the nature of what we are, not who we think we are.

Keep an open mind as long as you are not indecisive

Is an open mind a sign of curiosity, or are strong convictions a better sign of character?

Aging and death

Death is horrible enough, but undying consciousness is terrifying

THE ODD THING IS that I am optimistic even though I know it is illusory. Decline and death are inevitable but still, at an advanced age, far off in the future. I wonder if my optimism is a voluntary attitude.

Unless the growth of mind is arrested or is in the grip of an uncompromising idea, every decade in a creative life brings new challenges and possibilities. Paul Schilder said that death is always an interruption in a process of development, one that can be arranged in a series of stages. Thus, with sufficient longevity one traverses the twelve Nidānas of Buddhism (which extend from before birth to after death), and the eight stages of Erikson (which comprise natural signposts of a typical life,) but each stage demands a re-dedication, not just to persevere but to live creatively; to unearth meanings buried under shallow mounds, revive love grown stale, incite curiosity in least-noticed fragments, embrace the spiritual even if you profess immunity, seek windows of novelty in the cavern of the habitual, rejoice in the fresh taste of spring water over the reassuring palette of an aged wine.

Forgetting is the gift that makes real learning possible, which otherwise is a twig on the same shrub of knowledge, secreted away in an infinite library of countless volumes where a page or two is the sum of a life. The young are still searching at an age when Schubert was dying. Perhaps, they are seduced by the prospect of a long life when formerly, urgency was provoked by the specter of an early death. For many an early avocation or a summer job, temporary, transitional, grows into a rewarding and comfortable skill that shapes the ensuing years. One begins as a clerk and eventually owns the store. The surfer at middle age owns a surfboard shop. A year in religious training leads to fifty in the monastery. The apprentice becomes the master, never having to choose. A young friend said, wistfully, I wanted to write books, then I taught books, now I sell them. In my field, it is all too familiar to make a study of behavior or some part of the brain and continue unwavering for an entire career. Now, especially in the privileged, adolescence can last until thirty.

∞

Stages in life are not steps in a ladder; each is embedded in the next.

If a decline of the flesh accompanies a growth of the mind, do stages in life differ for bodily and mental aging?

The sine wave of bodily ascent and decline over the life span is mirrored in the arising and perishing of the mental state.

Dying is not eternal sleep or perpetual awakening, but dispersal to mulch for ensuing generations

We aim to be immortal but in death become ubiquitous.

Live long enough and see the spawn of Ozymandias sink into oblivion, meteors that sparkle as they perish, incinerated with others in the unwritten histories of the vast unremembered.

Look to the heavens but know that life is the firmament on earth.

Somewhere in my calendar on a date to be written is an appointment in Samarra, though I would rather go to the dentist.

Fate helps us to be courageous. If destiny is sealed, there is no fretting over inconsequential danger.

I have always feared dying before a book is finished, as if that was the only part of my life left incomplete

I feel things slipping away and try to hold on, drowning, clinging to driftwood

There is such a thing as the life force. I feel it dripping out of me

The monotony of aging makes the gambits of youth seem contrived.

It is hard to imagine that anything before this moment actually happened

More the pity that when I die a history will be lost

The soul is invented to fill a nothingness that defies contemplation

To think on death is for the color blind to imagine color

Unable to think outside mind we imagine death in relation to mind, such as eternal sleep or the self as soul.

If dying is oneness with matter, annihilation is release from separation.

If you favor population control and want to limit childbirth, the elderly should get out of the way.

Reflections on Mind and the Image of Reality

To return we all desire
In a form we hope is higher,
But if I come back as a cat
That is all there is to that

Endless awareness is hell, absolute extinction is heaven.
Curiosity keeps an old man alive, weariness kills him
Aging comes as a surprise, death as an interruption
The uninvited guest eventually shows up
We pass through life seeking reality; in dying, we meet the Absolute
Be alert at the very end as you degrade into matter or you will miss reality the instant of your death

Hartshorne thought the brain concentrates psychic particles that, in death, are released to the atmosphere. Similarly, the psychons of Eccles—each composed of its own unique mental experience—detach from the dendrons and scatter like mental dust. On its face, the idea is implausible. It is also hard, in such a view, to imagine an afterlife, but in holographic theory each particle can regenerate the whole.

Do not live to store up memories but to mitigate regret
Memories are the salve of aging, regret is the sting.

∽

Whatever form the soul may take
For me no difference can it make,
The horror of a fate infernal
Is continuance of mind eternal

The ashes of dead events, a crematory of incendiary remains, parts the gates of lives long past to scatter like shuttered birds
Cinders from a mortuary oven, then a candle on the Ganges
Vultures of Malabar take me to heaven,
Not maggots on earth in boxes of dung
Why live to the fullest? Die a little each day to lessen the finality that is coming.

Montaigne wrote, "to philosophize is to learn how to die".

The excitement that becomes the soft glow of memory is paltry recompense for the shrinking future of advancing age.

Adventures can be memorable but a new idea is thrilling.

With non-existence on either side, why should the soul continue after life is over but not before it begins?

Aging and death

Fechner thought we go from eternal sleep before birth, to half-wake, half-sleep in life, to eternal wakefulness after death. I prefer the reverse

Tears flowing for the loss of technique, she listened to a recording of a piano concerto 30 years ago. Young, we compare ourselves to others; older, to our former selves

Pack my trunk

I've lost my spunk

It's a race between illness and the doctors as to which will kill you first

I went blind in one eye from a retinal detachment reading Borges. My first thought was the irony he would appreciate that the reader goes blind reading a blind writer

The past is never left unsaved
A fingerprint on the face engraved

Aging was a bleak surprise
I could hardly believe my eyes
I woke one morning feeling old
As if my brain had turned to mold
Less the shrinking time ahead
More the life between instead

What echoes in my heart
Is the stillness of petals falling

If music without mind is noise, would beauty also disappear? What is the world if not a perspective? If the world is the sum of all perspectives, what will it lack minus my own?

What is a perspective without a self that perceives? If I relinquish my perspective, what happens to me?

The garden would suffer my cremation as a loss for the compost heap, a fine burial mound.

If we were down to one consciousness, and that disappeared, how would the world change? We assume it would be the same, but is that correct?

Mind elaborates the world but it is loss of the world I regret

An after-life is a ludicrous idea but what will I say to the angels?

The loss of memory matters only if we forget what never happened. The rest goes on without us. God give me the grace to return the gift of life in thankfulness.

Be silent on my passing. Converse with my books